DEDICATION

This book is for Denny, Megan, Rachel,
That Laurie, Rams, Cassandra . . . and every
knitter I ever met or corresponded with.
You taught me that knitting is not just a hobby,
but a destination. My life is infinitely richer
(and my stash infinitely better)
for knowing all of you.

Contents

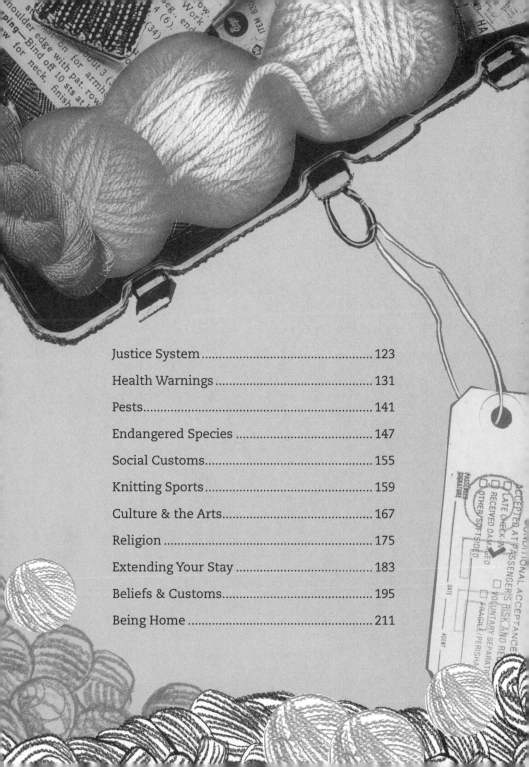

"It is not down in
any map; true
places never are."

— Herman Melville

INTRODUCTION

Wherever You Go, There You Are

EVEN IF YOU don't care to travel, if you're a knitter, you're on a journey to an amazing land. You packed your bags for this trip the first time you picked up needles and yarn, the first time someone showed you the knit stitch, or the first time you cracked open a knitting instruction book or surfed a knitting Web page.

For some people, the journey to this land is a spiritual one. These are the knitters who find serenity and relaxation in knitting (those who say knitting is the new yoga). For some, it is a journey of self-challenge. Those who view it this way seem to devour knitting, learning the way to cables and lace and grafting so quickly that you can scarcely stand to watch them without feeling inadequate. Some are drawn into knitting by the people they meet along the side of the road, and they are often changed, frequently inspired, and occasionally healed because of these encounters. (These are the most perplexing knitters for common humans to understand, and non-knitters try to avoid them at cocktail parties. You can guess how I know that.) Whatever the reason for embarking, however the journey can be characterized, or whatever you find when you get to the destination, the point is that knitting takes you on a journey — becoming a knitter is a process, and knitting itself is far, far more than a hobby. It's a destination, a location, a new land.

The land of Knitting is a remarkable place. Its borders are far-reaching, extending through almost every country in the world. (Admittedly, countries where it's about 100 degrees for much of the year have fewer Knitting ports of call, but surely you can understand how there might be just a smidge less incentive for warm knitting wear to develop in Zimbabwe than, say, Russia.) The land of Knitting has citizens residing all over the globe (and maybe on other planets too . . . nobody has ruled that out yet) and Knitting's denizens transcend borders, language, race, age, gender, fashion sense, and, to be entirely frank, occasionally intelligence.

Immigrants to the land of Knitting arrive by book, by video, with a mentor, in groups, alone . . . and sometimes lonely. They come in various states of confusion, trying to grapple with things that even we longtime residents still haven't entirely grasped. The currency (how much yarn is too much yarn?), the language (cast off or bind off?), the politics, the sports, the local customs: Citizens of the land of Knitting must navigate all of this bewilderment, usually while contending with those in the rest of the world, most of whom don't even believe in Knitting . . . at least, not as a destination.

Knitters have their own rules, their own society, and their own limits. How else can you explain millions and millions of people who understand that it's reasonable to buy an outrageous amount of yarn when you hear it's been discontinued, but that it's completely unreasonable to think you're going to finish knitting all of it before you die? How else do we all — millions of us, in every corner of the globe — know the password: "Just one more row"?

For a place where knitters spend so much time, we know very little about this remarkable land and its culture, and it's time we changed this. Welcome, then, to the first travel guide to the land of Knitting. We know you'll like it here, no matter who you are.

"All journeys have secret destinations of which the traveler is unaware."

— Martin Buber

POPULATION

THE LAND OF KNITTING is populated largely by people who didn't know they were coming here to live full time. They thought they were merely going to be tourists. They were just going to learn to knit or were just going to knit one or two things. They would pop in and out, vacation here, maybe contemplate a time-share condo . . . All knitters begin their journey through Knitting truly believing they're going to adopt knitting as a hobby or a skill, not a lifestyle.

In every Knitting immigrant's life there is a moment — different for each person — that sparked her interest in knitting and set her on this path. Maybe she saw a friend knitting or maybe she had a sudden remembrance of a relative who was a knitter. In those who are susceptible, simple exposure to wool products can trigger the knitting reflex. Perhaps a Knitting tourist begins by making only one baby blanket for an expected child or maybe just one fuzzy scarf to go with a favorite blue coat. Then, after finishing one scarf, she thinks that maybe some other people would like scarves too, and she makes more — and these people really like them. They think the knitter is very clever and the scarves are fun . . . and the knitter is still having tons of fun making them, so she knits even more scarves and everyone gets a scarf for Christmas (even that guy down the street whose name she doesn't know).

But then, one stunning day, the Knitting tourist thinks, "I have to stop knitting scarves. This is out of control. This can't go on. This much scarf knitting is not normal. Even the family dog has three scarves. I'm going to stop this madness right now." And she puts down the scarf yarn and walks away.

Then she takes a deep breath, and she looks around at the shape of her life and thinks about what it will be like now that she doesn't knit all the time. She tries to watch TV, but her hands feel itchy, and she tries simply to sit, but something is missing. She reminds herself that the scarves were madness, that the whole scarf-knitting episode was way gone to Crazyville — but then it suddenly comes to her in a flash of inspiration: She casts on for a hat . . . Whether she knows it or not, this innocent lady has just bought a nice little town house in the land of Knitting and has moved right in.

Caution: The One-Way Streeter

There exists in the land of Knitting a type of knitter who should be approached with caution: the One-Way Streeter. In the wild, the One-Way Streeter can be heard using words such as *always*, *never*, and the very intimidating *at no time*. This species is usually very good at knitting, with advanced skills . . . and one right answer. One-Way Streeters believe in one right way to do things — their way — and they can be very limiting when encountered by a brand-new resident. As teachers, they can be wonderful (if somewhat inflexible) guides to the things they know best. As mentors, their advice occasionally needs to be taken with a grain of salt.

If I say "Any way you want to turn the heel is fine — honestly, in knitting do whatever works for you" and you experience flushing, nausea, or anger, then you may be a One-Way Streeter. Try to loosen up a little.

Knitting Personality Types

The citizens of Knitting can be divided into many subcultures, but all of them fall into one of two broad categories: Process Knitters and Product Knitters. A Process Knitter knits for the sheer enjoyment of the activity, while a Product Knitter knits for the joy of the knitted stuff. The following quiz may help you identify both types in the wild and will help to clarify what type you are.

Note: Within the population, there are subgroups who blur the lines: Product Knitters who aren't willing to do some processes or Process Knitters who care about the products a great deal. Generally speaking, though, most knitters fit more into one category or the other.

Identifying Types of Knitters

The responses to the following situations will help clarify what type of knitter you are or what type you're dealing with.

1 It has become clear during the last several hours of knitting a project that you are not achieving gauge. In fact, this project has never heard of correct gauge and laughs with wild abandon in the face of gauge. Once you absorb that the project is very, very big/small/oddly shaped and you work your way through some language unbecoming a knitter, other knitters within earshot are most likely to hear you say:

Ⓐ "Screw it. Does anyone know a cold elephant? This has got to fit someone."

Ⓑ "My chest is 38 inches. This sweater is 37 ½ inches. This is never going to work. I'll start over. Sweaters are for wearing. "

2 This afternoon at the yarn shop there is a sale, and you buy a new pattern and some yarn to make a really keen sweater. You have with you a sweater that you are working on and you have two more under way at home. Knowing this full well, you:

Ⓐ Cast on the new sweater. What's the point of this question?

Ⓑ Put the bag with the new project in it beside your chair and keep working on the sweater you brought with you. Winter is coming and half sweaters don't keep anybody warm.

3 Your yarn shop offers knitting classes. You overhear the knitting teacher telling a whole class of students that they must knit, wash, and measure a swatch each and every time they begin a project. If you were teaching the class, you would say:

Ⓐ Sometimes swatches can be useful. (Then you would giggle a little.)

Ⓑ Exactly that. The teacher said it beautifully. The importance of swatches really can't be underscored enough. In fact, knit two big ones. You'll feel better.

4 If you had to write an essay about why you like knitting, you would:

Ⓐ Have trouble connecting with your feelings about knitting. I

mean, it's all intertwined, isn't it? The yarn, the feel of it, the beautiful stitches on the needle, the warm socks, how relaxed it makes
you feel, how excited it makes you feel, the cleverness of it all . . .
it's so hard to describe.

Ⓑ **Have trouble connecting** with your feelings about it. The yarn, the
sweaters, the elegance of a well-turned stitch, how clever you feel
as something comes off the needles, how proud you feel wearing
something you made yourself . . . it's so hard to describe.

5 You and your knitting friends are in a knitting store,
minding your own business, when the world's most beautiful
shawl practically reaches out and grabs you. You stop dead in
your tracks and look it in the eye. It's destiny. Its stitches know
your name and sing it to you. You don't wear shawls, however — in fact, no one you know wears shawls, and you can't
imagine making a new friend who wears shawls just to have
someone to give it to. Longingly you finger the stitches in your
hand and:

Ⓐ **Give the lady your credit card.** It doesn't matter if you have any
use for it or not. Just having created this thing of wonder will be
worth it and you're totally and completely enchanted by the idea
of trying something like this.

Ⓑ **Clutch at it,** think about it, wrack your brain for a purpose for it.
You imagine it as a wall hanging or just draped over the back of a
chair for the rest of your life or folded in your closet, but in the end,
you walk away . . . because knitted things are meant to be used.

This is what makes them wonderful, and if it has no use, it's not your kind of knitting.

If you had mostly A's: You are likely a Process Knitter. While you enjoy excellence in your work, you are flexible about it and it is the act of knitting that you really enjoy. If someone asked you what you love most about knitting, you would probably show her your favorite stitch or let her touch your softest yarn. You are the sort of knitter who would knit a square lace tablecloth for the same reason that mountain climbers ascend Everest: because it's there.

If you had mostly B's: You are likely a Product Knitter. You love to knit, and certainly don't knit only to get the stuff, but it is the thrill of finishing items and using them that keeps you on the job. You may be interested in trying new techniques, but there's just no way that you would knit mittens if all your friends lived in Jamaica.

Understanding the Resident Knitter

We knitters have been trying to help people understand what it is about knitting that moves us to be so passionate about it as a lifestyle. We keep telling them this: It's mostly fun, and when it's not fun, it's interesting.

This is not what people want to hear. If you tell them that these are your reasons for knitting, even if you get pretty excited

while you say it (and perhaps offer to let them hold your yarn and see if they feel anything warm and special), they will look at you (usually rather quizzically) and ask, "No, really . . . why do you knit? Isn't it the spirituality? Making things? Satisfying the human urge to create?" Then it gets tricky if you are the honest type, because you can knit for all of these reasons separately or none of them . . . or sometimes (rather painfully) all at once.

It is possible, even frequently probable, that knitting is deep. Many knitters speak of the meditative qualities of knitting, though the majority of us will collapse on the floor in a fit of giggles if you call knitting "the new yoga." (I've both knit and done yoga, and other than the occasional painfulness of both occupations, they don't have a lot in common.) Knitting isn't always meditative. Knitting isn't always fun. Knitting is sometimes meditative and knitting is often fun. It's also often challenging and often rewarding . . . but it's not always these. Knitting is also sometimes painful (both figuratively and literally; many of us can think of at least one knitter who has required a tetanus shot as a result of her knitting habit) and difficult, and this is the part that's hard to grasp.

From time to time, non-knitters who don't understand that some upset and frustration are part of the process of knitting have accused me of not really liking knitting as much as I think I do. (I can sort of understand how they might think that I'm not enjoying knitting when I've just whipped a half-knit sock at the wall while letting fly a string of filthy language.) When I get over

my initial shock at their statement, I realize the truth: *I don't like knitting. I love it* . . . and when you love something, you don't just give up on it the minute it stops being fun. (Most of us wouldn't still have our kids if that were the case.) You keep pursuing passions such as parenting, marriage, and knitting even when they aren't fun because they somehow fuel the human soul. Simply having a passion is a deep payoff, offering something more . . .

and
knitting
is like that.

The Essence of Knitting

A few years ago, I was in Ottawa and I had a profound experience. I met a woman (who will have to forgive me for forgetting her name), and she was doing something I had never considered, something that showed me that her trip to Knitting had taken a stunningly different road from mine: She collected plastic bags — ordinary plastic bags in a rainbow of colors from a variety of stores — and, using a sharp pair of scissors, she cut each bag into a long, continuous strip that sort of spiraled upward from the bottom of the bag. Then she took these long strips and wound them like balls of yarn. Once she had her colorways sorted out, she knit these strips into projects.

What was she knitting? What could possibly be worth this remarkable level of effort? She spent hours cutting up the bags, then hours knitting them, working out her stripes and (I swear it's true) Fair Isle patterns and making these bags into . . . bags. Tote bags that were very funky, bags that were much better than the original bags . . . but bags nonetheless. **Clearly these were bags with a higher calling**, but make no mistake: She spent hours and hours of work turning bags into bags.

I was astonished. It seemed so futile. It seemed . . . well, for maybe one minute I got a flash of how non-knitters see knitters. Then suddenly, right out of the blue, it occurred to me: This knitter was illustrating the true mysticism of knitting, the real answer, the response that people want us to give when they ask us why we knit, why people by the millions are driven to do it.

This woman had removed all the reasons I could think of for knitting. She wasn't having a tactile experience: She hadn't gone into a yarn shop and had a little falling down because she couldn't resist the thrill of how soft or beautiful the yarn was. Her "yarn" was just plastic. She wasn't doing it for the love of another person: She quietly confided to me that she was so taken with these bags that she was keeping every single one she made. She wasn't doing it for fashion: Bags made from bags have yet to turn up on the runways of Milan. She wasn't doing it out of time-honored responsibility, using her skills and needles to protect her family from the cold. She wasn't doing it because she needed a bag: She had tons of bags before she started.

This knitter had managed to remove from the equation all of the superficial reasons why people knit so that all that was left was the pure, unadulterated essence of knitting. Knitting is fun, it is interesting, and — here's the thing — it is an act of transformation.

It turns out that knitting isn't about the yarn or the softness or needing a hat (although we really can't argue with these secondary motivators). It's really about this: *Knitting is a magic trick.* In this day and age, in a world where science and technology take more and more wonder and work out of our lives and our planet is quickly becoming a place running out of magic, a knitter takes silly, useless string, mundane sticks, *waves her hands around* (many, many times . . . nobody said this was fast magic), and turns one thing into another: string into a hat, string into a sweater, string into a blanket for a baby. It really is a very reliable magic.

There is that thrilling moment when you finish something and you run your hands over it and your chest puffs up a little with an enormous, swelling pride and you desperately look around for someone you can explain your magic to, and when you find a person (best if it's someone you have met before), you hold your project out to him or her and *wait for the accolades to pour in.* This project represents hours of your life. This knitting is cleverness, patience, intelligence . . . this piece of work is impressive, darn it, and you show it to the spectator with a glowing face and bursting heart, and you wait for him or her to get it.

When (not if, but when) the someone you choose to show it to isn't as impressed with your spectacular knitting as you think he or she should be, I can't be the only one who is so offended by this lack of understanding that I want to wag the ball of yarn wildly in the face of my detractor and scream, "LOOK! Look at this! This [here I hoist the yarn aloft] is what I started with. *It's yarn!* This [here I wildly wave the finished socks with my other hand] is what I have now! Socks! Socks are nothing like yarn! *You can't wear yarn!* Yarn isn't socks! I made something you can wear out of yarn! Look at this, praise me, and know the wonder that is a knitter!"

For the record, this approach has never worked well. Only the citizens of Knitting know the truth: While knitting is fun and interesting, it's the magic trick, the magic act of transformation that is the answer to the question *"Why do you love knitting?"*

May 10

Dear Mum,

You were right about the new apartment. The place isn't so bad once you get some paint on the walls and go looking for your good attitude. I think that I like it more now that Andy's got some of the pictures up too. It makes it seem more "ours." This afternoon, I finished with the living room and walked down the street to the bookstore. I know, I know: I finally finish unpacking all of the books only to go and buy more.

The shop is nice, and they have a really good magazine section. While I was looking around, though, I saw the funniest thing: There was a group of women in the café part of the store, sitting in a circle, drinking coffee, chatting, hanging out . . . and Mum, they were all knitting, the whole bunch of them, just knitting away! At first, I thought it was a coincidence, then I thought no way — that many people wouldn't all be knitting at the same time unless it was arranged. But who would arrange something like that?

I couldn't stop looking at them, but I didn't want them to know I was staring so I just stood behind a display of woodworking books. I don't think they saw me. I've always thought knitting was sort of a solitary thing — you know, evenings in front of the TV . . . In the end, I figured this group had to be some kind of a trippy club.

One woman was working on something blue (a nice blue, sort of like the color of that chesterfield we used to have downstairs), and all of a sudden she tossed it on the floor and said really loudly, "That's it! I quit knitting!" Then all of her friends laughed and sho__ their heads as though it was the funniest thing they had ever heard, and one of them said, "Oh yeah!" and another one said, "Like you could!" Then they all laughed and laughed again and she picked u__ the knitting and kept going.

It was like some weird cult. I bought a book of poems and left, but I keep thinking about those crazy ladies.

Love,
Alice

From: knittiest@synenet.knit
Subject: Thanks for the yarn
Date: May 10 10:26:48 PM EDT
To: kmarg@symport.knit

Hi Marg,

I just wanted to thank you again for bringing me that yarn this afternoon. I took a look at that pattern when I got home and I'll have enough when I add together the two amounts. I love the design enough that I would have chanced it, but now I feel really confident. I'm a big fan of extreme knitting, but I'm getting sick of the style of my stuff being dictated by how much yarn I have. Half of my sweaters have ¾-length sleeves and the other half have "emergency stripes." I have got to learn to buy that extra skein (or ten)!

As an aside, did you see that woman staring at us from behind the stacks in the bookshop? I almost invited her over, but she looked so spooked that I thought we might just scare her more. I bet she's a knitter. She may not know it yet, but I just bet.

See you next week. Thanks again for the stash enhancement.

Liv

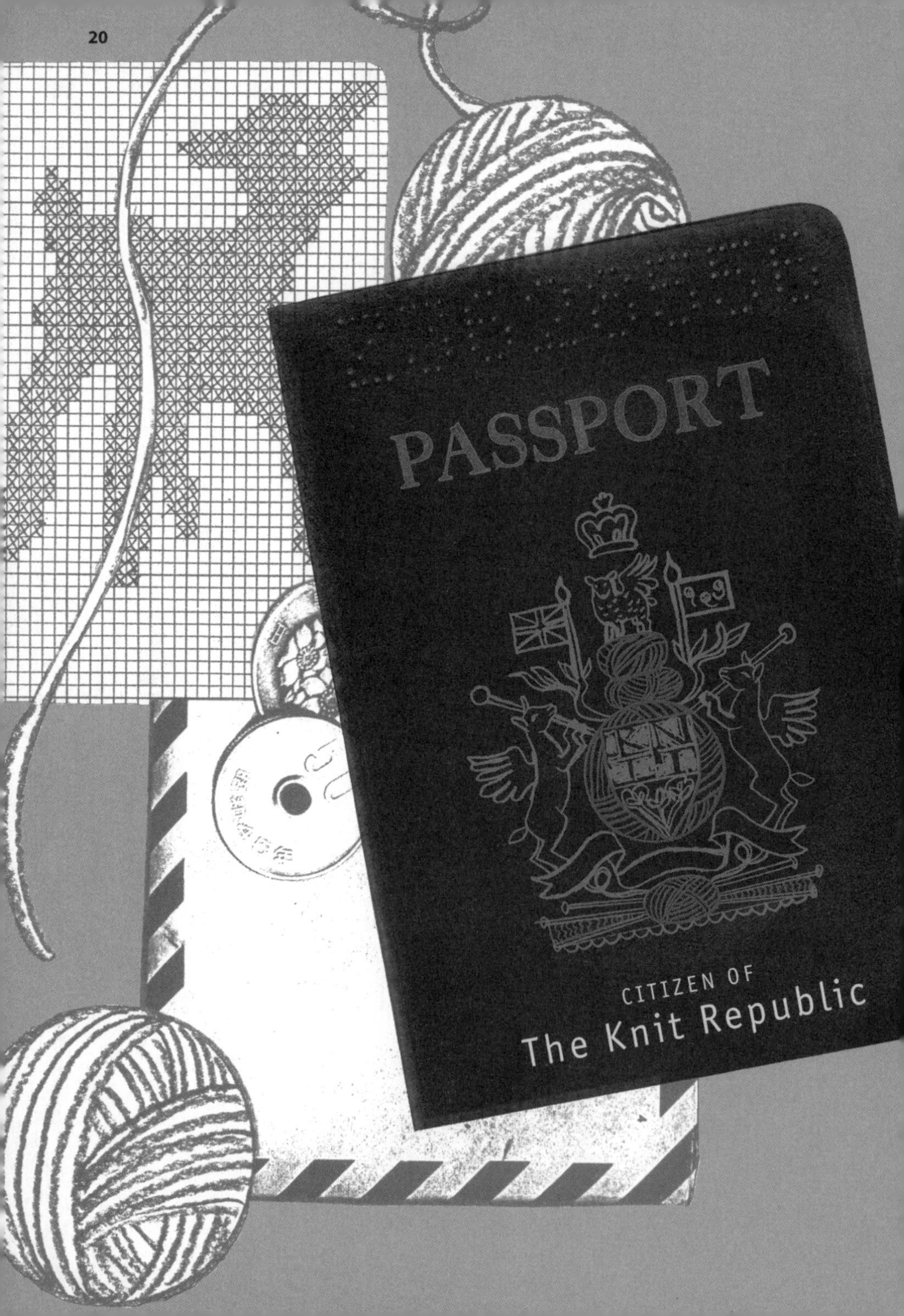
PASSPORT
CITIZEN OF
The Knit Republic

Greeting the Citizens of Knitting

In North America you might be greeted with a hug or a handshake; in China, a slight bow; in France, kisses on both cheeks. The Japanese put their heels together and bow with their hands on their thighs, while in India you may be greeted with hands together at chest level.

In the land of Knitting, do not be alarmed when knitters greet you by stroking, touching, fondling, or examining the clothing you are wearing. The mildest form of this greeting is a quick touch at the cuff of your sweater, while some bolder residents may approach from behind and grasp your shawl with both hands, perhaps making an exclamation such as *"Ohhh! Is this silk?"* This is natural behavior for knitters and is a sign of respect and welcome. In addition to the greeting function, the interest in your outfit may relate to the fact that you're wearing something hand-knit or something greeters think might be hand-knit, that it's made from a fiber they would like to knit with, or that the garment may be something they think they could turn into a hand-knit by duplicating it if they could get a close enough look. Occasionally, a knitter carries a sketchbook for the purpose of recording cables and interesting stitch patterns, and this note-taking and quick sketching of your outfit is also normal and complimentary, as is stalking complete strangers to get a look at their hats.

Similarly, do not be surprised when you discover this impulse in yourself. It doesn't take long to learn the customs. Running your hand down the sleeve of a fellow knitter's sweater when you meet him or her is a healthy expression of knitterly interest and is not at all odd.

It's the knitter's handshake. (Just in case you get around, I should warn you that the spinner's handshake and the weaver's handshake are also quite aggressive.)

TOURISM OFFICES, OR
WHO ENDS UP HERE
AND WHY CAN'T WE CONVINCE
EVERYONE TO COME?

WHEN I BEGAN THINKING about the idea of Knitting as a
destination or a journey, I gave some thought to how difficult
it is to explain to non-knitters the many and varied charms of
the land of Knitting. Despite the fact that (and I really am sure
of this) non-knitters do other things for fun, such as play team
sports, golf, garden, or fly-fish, the uninitiated seem particularly
perplexed by our fascination with knitting.

I've tried to figure out why it's possible for the yarnless
masses to accept watching movies as a valid hobby but to
see knitting as unimaginative and stodgy and as emotionally
enriching as licking stamps. Is it knitting's association with
women and thus some sort of old-fashioned sexism that says
that anything feminine can't be significant? Is it our stashes? I
understand that if you don't fear the possibility that your favorite yarn could be discontinued or that all sheep could go bald,
hoarding wool as knitters do could seem a little silly. (It would
seem sillier, perhaps, if half the people in North America didn't
have basements and garages full of old magazines and clothing
that doesn't fit them, but I digress.) Perhaps it is the sense of
community knitters can have, the clubs and guilds where knitters gather and do . . . what? Just knit? Although the knitter's
tendency to gather in flocks flies in the face of the traditional

idea of a grandmother knitting alone in her living room, there is a gathering for every hobby, from quilt shows to *Star Trek* conventions. Knitters aren't the only individuals to seek out the company of their peers. Once you've accepted that a Klingon language seminar can exist, there shouldn't be any trouble getting your head around a Tuesday Knit Night.

"The traveler was active; he went strenuously in search of people, of adventure, of experience. The tourist is passive; he expects interesting things to happen to him. He goes 'sight-seeing.'"

— Daniel J. Boorstin

Tourist or Traveler?

I've been both, and making your way through Knitting is no better one way than the other. In fact, most knitters flip back and forth, the same way that some people will take a hike on one day of their vacation, discovering nooks and crannies of the culture, and spend the next day lying on the beach with a nice bit of cotton knitting and a mai tai. There's no shame in either pursuit.

Which are you, tourist or traveler?

A tourist says: I'm making the sweater on page 6 of that magazine. I always love that designer's patterns.

A traveler says: I'm making the same one, except I'm shortening the arms, making the body longer, putting in shaping at the waist, adding a cable at the top, and taking off the collar. Her stuff is just great, isn't it?

GETTING THERE:
TRAVELING TO KNITTING

THERE ARE MANY WAYS to journey to the land of Knitting. What road are you taking to get there? Look at your responses to the following situations and learn your Knitting journey style.

1 You've suddenly discovered a big mistake in your latest sweater. You haven't cast off yet and there's still a chance that you could go back and fix it. Your reaction is:

Ⓐ **I don't mind. Nobody's perfect,** and I wouldn't have that really unique triangle sweater with the great elbow lumps if it weren't for those extra decreases I invented.

Ⓑ **I'm going to try to live with it.** I'll think about fixing it, I'll actually think about fixing it with every row that I knit between now and when I finish, but ultimately, I won't bother . . . and I won't wear the sweater, either. I'll finish it and sew it up and block it, but that mistake will stare me down each and every time I try to put it on.

Ⓒ **I'm absolutely ripping it back** and having another go. (Probably at 3 a.m. because I can't sleep knowing that there's a mistake in it. As a matter of fact, I don't have time for this quiz.)

Ⓓ **Hey, do you think I could turn this into a bathrobe** if I made the same mistake on the back?

2 On an ordinary Thursday Knit Night, a new knitter comes. You notice that the three inches of scarf she's knitting has all of the cables going in the wrong direction, although she's thrilled with it. You:

(A) **Congratulate her** on her newfound knitting skills, get her a cupcake, and welcome her warmly. Isn't it great that she's knitting?

(B) **Welcome her warmly** but find it impossible not to mention the, um . . . creative approach. After biting your tongue for a while, you ask her if she's doing it on purpose and if not, whether she would like you to help her fix it.

(C) **You wait for her to go to the bathroom** and fix them all. You have to. It's the only way to get rid of the twitchy eye that you develop whenever you're around big knitting errors.

(D) **Go over and watch her closely.** Maybe she's onto something.

3 Mary is knitting a lace shawl. As she knits across the row, everything is perfect and the pattern is lining up beautifully. At the end of the row, however, there's a single leftover stitch. Your advice to Mary is:

(A) **Knit two together. See?** It's the right number of stitches again. Pass the cake!

(B) **Un-knit the row** and see if you can find your mistake. If a thing is worth doing, it's worth doing well.

(C) **Get out the graph paper,** rechart the row, and see if you can locate the error. If you can't, compare your chart with the original and look for anomalies. If you find one, you should get a calculator and rechart the row to correct the error and deal with your leftover stitch. If you don't find an anomaly, write to the designer to advise her of the error in her chart.

Ⓓ **Increase again!** Make it have wings!

④ After an hour in the yarn shop looking for the perfect pattern, you're forced to admit defeat. The pattern you're looking for just doesn't exist there. While you are sad about this turn of events, you decide to move on with your life. (Remember, this is just a quiz; we're skipping over the part where you have a bit of a fit before gracefully deciding to give up.) Your thoughts are:

Ⓐ **Hey! New sock yarn!**

Ⓑ **This one is close.** Maybe if I shorten the sleeves and add a little width, this pattern could work.

Ⓒ **Why do I have to do everything myself?** Somebody get me my calculator, graph paper, and sketchbook. I don't need a pattern; I can totally figure this out.

Ⓓ **This is a great opportunity** to make that free-form spiral cape I was thinking about.

If your responses are mostly A's: You are traveling to the land of Knitting on a cruise. You don't care how you get there or what sort of things you produce while you're there, and you don't stay up nights regretting the sloppy decrease you did on that sweater sleeve. You're in it for the good time and you're Knitting's answer to blender drinks by the pool. People on another kind of trip through Knitting often look at you and your happiness and relaxed demeanor and wish that they weren't compelled to worry as much as they do about that cable that doesn't look quite right. On the other hand, they don't wonder why your end results are a little unpredictable (if that's what we're calling that last hat you knit that could double as a beach bag if you turned it upside down and added a handle).

If your responses are mostly B's: Your path to Knitting is a good old-fashioned road trip. You've got some maps and you're pretty sure where the motel is, but if you see a sign for a cool roadside attraction, you're absolutely taking the exit ramp for the afternoon. Your fellow knitters admire your balanced approach and steady progress and the way that most of your knitwear fits and is human-shaped. (We're overlooking the items that didn't work out — the ones you've stuffed in the back of the closet. We won't tell.) Your strong suit is how reasonable you are about your knitting. You are the middle ground and your sanity is pretty safe.

If your responses are mostly C's: Get out of the way, baby, because you're traveling on a space-age monorail that's never late. You are accurate and deliberate, methodical and clear-thinking, and other knitters dream of turning out the work that you do. You can tell a right-leaning decrease from a left-leaning one and you can think of four ways to make a buttonhole. Your work is beautiful because you are a perfectionist and you work hard to get things right. You believe that most people could knit as well as you if only they would work as hard as you, and you're right, though it would help if they also had your obsessive streak.

If your responses are mostly D's: You, my dear knitter, are a skydiver. You're Knitting's daredevil, and if anyone is going to learn anything by living it, it's you. Your knitting is wild and adventurous, and though the rest of us never think your ideas are going to work out, they usually do. You are the knitter who reminds all of us not to take it so seriously (and you drive the type C knitters nuts). You are the knitting world's mad adventurer, and the only downfall to your "go big or go home" approach is that, much as with literal skydiving, your mistakes tend to be fantastically bad. Luckily, this doesn't bother you, because on the way to your last crash-and-burn project, you discovered a new, really stretchy cast-on.

"Travel is fatal to prejudice, bigotry, and narrow-mindedness, and many of our people need it sorely on these accounts. Broad, wholesome, charitable views of men and things cannot be acquired by vegetating in one little corner of the earth all one's lifetime."

— **Mark Twain**

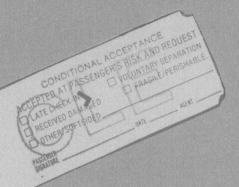

CONDITIONAL ACCEPTANCE
ACCEPTED AT PASSENGER'S RISK AND REQUEST
LATE CHECK-IN   ☐ VOLUNTARY SEPARATION
☐ RECEIVED DAMAGED   ☐ FRAGILE/PERISHABLE
☐ OTHER/SOFTSIDED
DATE _____   AGENT _____
PASSENGER
SIGNATURE _____

PACKING TIPS FOR TRAVELING TO KNITTING

Things to bring with you when you go to
Knitting

- **A sense of humor.** When good knits go bad — and good knits do go bad, no matter how careful or skilled the knitter — you have two choices: You can either laugh yourself stupid (a sweater with arms that long really is funny) or you can get all bent out of shape with the seriousness of it. It's your choice, but let me tell you, I've done it both ways and when I was finished with the woolly temper tantrum, the arms of my sweater were still way too long.

- **Flexibility.** That yarn just doesn't come in the blue you want and you're never going to get gauge with that worsted weight. Move on.

- **An appreciation for the element of surprise.** It is possible — and I have had more proof of this than I could ever express to you — to plan knitting down to the finest detail. You can take classes, you can swatch, you can carefully measure gauge and even wash the swatch before you take its gauge. All measures can be taken, all cautions heeded, all processes can be as thoughtful and deliberate as though you were launching a space shuttle. Experts can be consulted throughout, techniques can be researched, and accuracy can be ascertained. Then, after all the planning and thorough regard . . . your sweater can suck and you will never know why. The element of surprise is an indelible part of knitting.

- **Respect for the unknown.** Gauge. Enough said.
- **Curiosity.** I have been knitting for thirty-four years, and recently a woman who has been knitting for almost seventy years showed me something that she learned at a class taught by a twenty-two-year-old. Curiosity in knitting breeds adventure.

Things to leave at home

- The idea that you will always be perfect
- The concept that if you get really good at it, knitting will be predictable
- Any thought you may have had about there being only one right way to do this, any idea in your head of what a knitter looks like, and any hope that you will ever have enough storage space in your home

"One's destination is never a place, but a new way of seeing things."

— **Henry Miller**

Five Ways
That Knitting Is Easier than the Real World

1. **Unlike with my family** or coworkers, I can demand that a sock be perfect. I can do it over and over again, holding it to the highest standard. The sock has no self-esteem for me to damage and will never go into therapy if I say out loud that it's a terrible sock that no one would ever want.

2. **I can give up** on a project for no reason at all and nobody will think that I lack commitment or a sense of loyalty.

3. **I can rip back** a lace scarf, erasing all my errors and pretending to all the world that I never knit it, and unlike at my job, no one will ever ask me what the hell I spent last week doing.

4. **I can knit as much** or as little as pleases me in a day, completely according to my whim. There is no supervisor who will check on my productivity.

5. **I can have six projects** on the go at once, love and enjoy them all as individuals, dump one and take up with another, and not be at all worried what my mother will think of me when she finds out I'm this unfaithful.

August 6

Hey Deb!

I'm so glad to hear from you! I really miss you guys. If I called you every time I thought of you, we'd be on the phone all day and the phone company would be able to buy every employee a new car.

This move has been even more of a big change than I thought it would be. Andy's working ridiculous hours at his new job, and now that the apartment's set up and I'm not getting lost on my way to work every day, I'm a bit at loose ends. Mum keeps encouraging me to try to meet people, but you know what I'm like. When I miss all of you, I end up reverting to type and hanging out in the bookstore by my house. Books can be good places to find friends when you're short of them. (Though I admit that you and Grace are better conversationalists.)

It turns out that I found more than I was expecting. The very first time I went down to the shop I saw a group of women knitting. I figured it had to be a club or something, and I thought about it for a while after I saw them. Have you ever seen a group of people together and just seeing what a good time they're having together makes you sort of lonely? I think it's the contrast. These women reminded me of how the three of us hung out at Java's back East. I found myself keeping an eye out for them, stopping by the bookstore on my way home . . . hanging around the place, waiting to see them.

When I went back to the store the tenth time, it hit me that I was stalking a knitting group. Who stalks knitters? How bored do you have to be to follow knitters around? It suddenly hit me that maybe I needed something to do. Maybe I needed an interest, a hobby, maybe I should try being interested in knitting instead of knitters. It seemed more sane, and I grabbed a "learn to knit" book off the shelf and tore out of there.

The book just sat for a couple of days until Saturday.

Andy was working (again) and I had run out of things to do. (That I alphabetized the cookbooks was a hint that I was hitting a low point.) While I was cleaning up the bedroom, I put my hand on the knitting book. I looked at it and it looked back at me and I thought, "Why not?" Why the hell not? At least learning to knit would be a way to fill up an evening. I looked up "knitting" in the Yellow Pages and went to a yarn store.

The irony hit me immediately: Here I'd been stalking the knitters in the bookstore, and where were they? You guessed it. The yarn shop has a huge table in the back, and at least ten people (two of them were guys) were sitting around the table, knitting and laughing. A lady got up when I came in and asked me if I needed any help, and I don't even know what I said. It all happened pretty fast after that. There was yarn, then there were needles, then someone offered me a chair and asked me what I was going to make.

I stared at the lady who'd asked the question, then I stared at the yarn and needles I'd just bought . . . and I realized that I'd left the stupid book on the table at home and this whole thing was going to be like Invasion of the Body Snatchers when they all point and scream "NOT ONE OF US!" But they didn't. I looked her in the eye and said, "I don't know. I think I'm just starting and I don't know whether or not I'm a knitter."

When I said that, the lady beside me put her hands on mine and said, "Sure you are. You're going to be good at this." She took the yarn and needles, and she put loops on one of the needles and showed me the knit stitch, and then she showed me again (and again and again), and then I knit. I knit for two hours in that shop, and then I knit for two more hours when I got home (I think it might be addictive).

When Andy came home, I was sitting in the living

room hunched over this crooked, funny bit of knitting. He cocked his head sideways and he just stared at me for a while, then he asked me what I was making. I told him the truth: I wasn't making anything — just a blue square of wonky knitting — and he laughed and said, "That's a pretty funny project, Alice!" It hit me that he was right. When he went into the kitchen, it also hit me that I might be wrong. I might not be making a blue square. Those women had invited me back for next Saturday. Maybe the square wasn't what I was making. Maybe I was making friends.

Either way, this knitting thing might be interesting.

Kiss the kids for me.

Alice

(P.S. Does the knitting thing make me a dork?)

NOTABLE KNITTER

Debbie New

Debbie New, an innovative knitter and a tremendous creative force, sports a fascinating résumé. Biomedical engineer, writer, teacher, violinist, inventor, potter, and, probably most staggeringly, a mother of eight, Debbie knits as though there are absolutely no limits to what knitting can do. This is probably because — in her hands, at least — this is absolutely true. Debbie has used knitting to create a seaworthy lace coracle (a small boat), a ticking grandfather clock, a portrait of her grandmother (using garter stitch and some cubist concepts), detailed teacups, a knitterly Madonna and Child, perfect seashells, figures, an extraordinarily long strip with turns in it that somehow folds into a jacket, and much more that nobody expects knitting to do.

Debbie New takes knitting to a place where you wouldn't expect to find it and in so doing opens doors through which all of us can walk. After all, if this woman can knit a boat that floats, surely you can turn the heel of a sock.

Five Things
to Tell a Recent Immigrant to Knitting

1 **You're not defusing a bomb.** At some point early in her time in Knitting, each potential citizen can be found gripping the needles, white-knuckled, brow furrowed, creating all kinds of new worry lines on her face while keeping a tighter hold on the working yarn than a drowning person has on her life raft. These new knitters need perspective. Nobody can knit well with that level of anxiety. Should you see one of these tense travelers, it will benefit her enormously to approach her slowly (and not from behind; she's wound up pretty tight), touch her shoulder, and gently say, "You're not defusing a bomb."

2 **Everybody starts like an idiot.** Nobody can knit the first row out of the gate. It's like anything else: Dating, dancing, holding a baby — it all feels horribly awkward and dorky at first, but it gets better. You've just got to hang in there long enough for the magic to start. (In the interest of complete honesty, that might be awhile. Hang in.)

3 **We all knit crap.** You can be knitting for twenty years and still turn out occasional crap. It's true that the longer you knit, the less crap you knit, but it never goes away entirely. Don't quit because of the crap.

4 **Don't knit with bad yarn.** Start with something you really love to touch. What you end up with can be only as good as what you start with. Yarn is reusable. You can have a do-over.

5 **Some level of obsession is normal.** Don't worry if you can't seem to stop knitting or thinking about knitting or wondering when you can knit again. It means you've arrived.

IDENTIFYING
CONSULATES AND EMBASSIES

THERE ARE STATIONS IN KNITTING that are there to
help and guide you, no matter how lost you become. I used to
be a solitary knitter, sitting in my house by myself and struggling quietly on my journey through Knitting. I was passionate
about knitting. I loved it very much and I'd been doing it a long
time, but it had never occurred to me that there were others out
there, pockets of hope and camaraderie, bastions of support and
nourishment where you can admit that sometimes you think
about rolling around in cashmere while scantily clad and the
people around you look at you and nod and sigh in agreement
instead of back away slowly without making any sudden moves
in your direction. Knitters need an outlet of peers, and ordinary
people don't cut it. I'm not sure how many times I've tried to
force complete strangers into a discussion about knitting, but
I think I could make an educated guess based on the fact that
the party invitations have dried up over the years. Finding your
local embassies and consulates is a good idea — for all parties
concerned.

A *consulate* is a nation's office in a foreign country that is
responsible for taking care of the rights and privileges of its na-
tionals in that country. It issues visas, helps travelers in trouble,
and helps them find their stuff if they've lost it.

You know you've found a consulate representing the land of
Knitting when you see someone in the park knitting a sock, or
when a knitter on the bus lends you a darning needle because

you can't find yours, or when an older man tells you about the techniques used in sock knitting during the war to save wool, or when the knitter who bought the same blue yarn as you did on sale gives you some just because you ran out. All of these people are Knitting's consuls, and you can find them all over the world — on buses, in plumbing stores, in restaurants while you wait for takeout and work on a half-knit sock. Any knitter out in public could be a consulate.

At a guild once I witnessed a very touching moment: An elderly woman sat beside a young, tattooed girl and both of their heads were bowed over some knitting in a clear moment of teaching. I was totally inspired by this. I reflected on the beauty of the older generation passing on an entire lifetime of wisdom and experience. In fact, I was getting a little weepy about it when I happened to overhear them. The girl was teaching the old woman her first cast-on, and I learned a pretty good lesson about accepting consulates where you find them and however they look. Stereotyping is only going to slow you down and make you miss some.

An embasssy is a bigger deal than a consulate. Sure, it still takes care of knitters abroad, and, like consulates, the ground an embassy sits on is official soil of the land of Knitting, but embassies also provide other services, and they represent Knitting's economy, trade, and international relationships. There are a few exceptions, but usually an embassy looks a lot like a yarn shop.

Services You Can Usually Find at an
Embassy

- **A swift and ball winder** you can use (assuming you bought the yarn there, or that you have bought so much yarn there in the past that the yarn shop owner named her third child after you).

- **Reasonable pattern support** (provided you bought the yarn there).

- **Help substituting yarns.**

- **Reasonable emotional support.** Crying (a lot) is not reasonable, though everybody's going to understand if you're crying about the gauge thing or if you ran out of yarn.

- **Use of a calculator** for the purposes of on-site yarn substitution and alchemy.

- **Calling a taxi** for you if you buy more than you can carry home on foot.

- **Emergency emotional help for the stranded knitter.** Should you find yourself lonely, lost, or at loose ends in any town in the world, a yarn shop is almost always a good place to start looking for a friend.

Useful Translations

I'm going for a walk.
I'm going for a walk to a yarn shop.

Would you like to go for a drive?
The yarn shop I want to go to is too far for walking.

On the way there, do you mind if we make a stop? *There's another yarn shop between here and there.*

I hear that New York is wonderful.
I hear it has a lot of yarn shops.

I'm going to a yarn shop.
Shut your mouth; it beats my having an affair.

I'm going shopping.

I'm going to a yarn shop.

Embassy Etiquette

Yarn shops can and will answer quick knitting questions for almost anyone, but how much is determined by the rules of polite behavior. There is etiquette to be observed on both sides.

If you purchased the project at the shop, it is reasonable to expect the shop to provide a certain amount of help to complete it. A request to demonstrate a particular decrease or a two-minute explanation of a pattern term should always be no problem.

If a knitter experiences severe knitting problems that are taking a great deal of time to solve, it is considered appropriate for the shop to suggest a class or a fee. (Some yarn shops offer unlimited help with your project, but only during specific hours when there is a staff member available to assist you.) It is not okay to take up a billion hours of a shop owner's or employee's time with a problem that's out of control. As much as yarn shops feel like home to us, they are actually businesses. (Stunning, but true.)

It is considered very poor form for a knitter to bring in a project that was purchased at another shop and demand help. You may request help, but free help when another store turned the profit should never be the expectation.

Note: The finest yarn shops make exceptions based on humanitarian need. Crying knitters are frequently sorted out regardless of where they purchased their yarn. If your wool has been so cruel as to reduce you to helpless sobs, stagger to a yarn shop. Someone will lift you up.

CONSULATES & EMBASSIES

"Good company
in a journey
makes the way seem shorter."

— Izaak Walton

Have you ever . . . ?

- **Tried to teach your children to knit** not because you want them to develop the skill, but so that you'll be able to discuss one-row buttonholes with them?

- **Told your spouse "Knitting is dead sexy"** or "You look hot with that yarn," which (while very true) is really only a ploy on your part to get him to play knitting games with you?

- **Seen someone else knitting in public** and tried really hard to go over and talk to her about it, but failed out of shyness? (Double points if you tried to see exactly what she was knitting without her noticing you lurking behind her.)

- **Thought that it would be really great if there was yarn** at parties?

- **Noticed that when you go upstairs excitedly** to show your wife that you finally figured out how to knit a cable and it looks absolutely fabulous, she's suspiciously hard to wake up?

- **Realized that every time you sneak** in just a little discussion about sock heels at social events, the person you're talking to suddenly sees somebody she really has to talk to on the other side of the room?

If you've answered **yes** to any of these questions, then you need to find some knitters.

Three Ways
to Get Knitting Friends

1. **Give birth to them.** This is the slow way. Most kids raised by knitters do learn to knit eventually, but many of them give it up during their teen years, when they would rather die than be anything like you. They'll probably come back to it.

2. **Create them out of the friends** you already have. Start by making them a few beautiful things to get them hooked, then withdraw the supply exactly when the snow begins to fly.

3. **Go where the knitters are.** Check out guilds, shops, clubs, and the Internet. Look for the people holding yarn.

CONSULATES & EMBASSIES

GATHERING PLACES: WHERE TRAVELERS IN KNITTING MEET

IT'S A VERY GOOD IDEA for knitters to find themselves a few traveling companions. Getting on the buddy system, however you choose to do it, can encourage even wider travel in Knitting, and it's way, way easier than you think. I've been in Knitting embassies and consultates all over North America and I'm always completely astonished at how knitting can unite the strangest combinations of people. Politics, religion, age, gender, status, and sexual orientation are suddenly unimportant. Knitters who would normally mix as well as champagne and Spam are suddenly getting along like . . . well, like people who have a whole lot in common. Knitting melts the usual barriers and leaves people free to strike up unlikely friendships. The secret is finding the magic group for you.

Never Again Knit Alone

Not that I would ever advocate knitting as the sole treatment for mental illness (especially for some of us who collect yarn and patterns in a way that indicates the seeds of an obsessive-compulsive disorder), but the land of Knitting and the people who inhabit it provide ample evidence that Knitting, whether you visit the place or or live there, can definitely influence the path of your emotional life.

There are many knitters — and I count myself among them — who have found that not just Knitting, but also the citizens of the place, can provide ample relief from advanced cases of loneliness, mild cases of depression, and chronic underappreciation of the knitterly habit. There are those of us who once were the only knitters in our social circles and families and were chronically misunderstood and thought strange. (The ways of yarn and needle do not always seem clear to those who do not understand.) I was the only person I knew who knit for the soul, who took endless joy in wool and needles and making something from them. I was the only person I knew who found that knitting simply made people happier, more patient, more engaged, and more interested, and that, for better or worse (for crazy or sane), knitting was not just a hobby, but an element of my personality. Stumbling into the world of knitters was remarkable. Even though I tend to be shy and nervous around new people, with knitters I always have a conversation starter, a beginning. This is often enough to help me find out if I like someone. Many of my best friends are knitters, and only because we had our mutual love of the act to serve as a first step. Once you find your way to the land of Knitting and knitters, you may discover the friends of your heart, the people who feel as you do and do as you do, and that can transform lives.

Caution: Dangers of Social Knitting

Developing a social network of knitters can often lead to social knitting, which occurs within a pack of knitters who are gathered together in the wild. Knitters are frequently surprised to discover, however, that a Knit Night, despite being the only night of the week or month set aside explicitly for this activity, is frequently the least productive of all knitting times. **Reasons include:**

- **Talking.** Talking slows down knitters engaged in anything but the most simple projects. Even knitters working on garter-stitch scarves will notice time lost to gesturing with knitting needles to make a point.

- **Eating.** Many social events include food. Because it is still so-cially unacceptable to put your face in a plate and gnaw in an ovine fashion, eating and fork handling chew up knitting time.

- **Drinking.** Aside from the seconds lost to sipping (although a long straw can solve access issues), many social events include alcohol, and its effects are often devastating to knitters. Among these consequences is having to pick back each and every row accomplished while under the influence and, worse, while hung over. Knitting setbacks are painful enough without having to admit that you have no one to blame but yourself. Drink moderately or lower your risk by knitting garter stitch. Either way, remember that friends don't let friends knit drunk.

Gender Distinctions in Knitting

Sadly, Knitting is definitely a land with a gender gap. There certainly are men who knit, men who knit well, men who design knits, and men hanging out in yarn shops, but it is still true, at least in this time in history, that knitting is largely a feminine pursuit, despite the fact that historically and traditionally, knitting was done almost exclusively by men.

Why should men knit?

•Men who take up knitting in North America will be surrounded by women. If I were a single guy looking for good odds, I'd live at the yarn store.

•Because people don't see many men knitting, they tend to be really impressed and taken with the men they do see. Attention for a male knitter is like white on rice. (I once held my tongue for about ten painful minutes while some woman gushed all over my buddy's garter-stitch scarf and ignored my Orenburg shawl. I, like most female knitters, have tried not to be at all bitter about this.)

•Samurai, the least feminine of men, were known to knit. At the zenith of the samurai's power and status, they earned all their income from being professional warriors, but as having a bunch of warriors standing around fell out of fashion in Japan, many samurai took up knitting — first as a cost-saving measure, to make their own gloves and socks, and then to supplement their income.

- We always talk about how men would make better spouses, partners, and parents if they had more focus, attention to detail, and patience. Knitting's pretty good for helping you to acquire these skills.

- Knitting is dead sexy (for both genders).

Guilds

Guilds are like clubs for knitters, but they usually have an educational focus as well as a social one. Guilds have a long history and began as unions for knitters. The guilds would train and evaluate knitters, set a price for an individual's work, and use their numbers to buy materials in bulk to save money. Usually, members pay a small amount to join and attend meetings every month or so. Guilds have committees that organize guest speakers, teachers, trunk shows, visits from yarn companies, and ways for knitters to share skills. These entrances to the land of Knitting are like universities, except that everyone can go, most of the "professors" are pretty darned cool, you don't have to know anything when you get there, and there's a party (however restrained) at every class. (Now that I think about it, maybe how much they are like universities depends on what university you attended.) No matter how new or experienced a knitter may be, everyone who pays his or her dues is welcome at a guild.

Clubs and Groups

Clubs are a lot like knitting guilds, but they offer more parties and less formal education. If guilds are Knitting's universities, clubs are the fraternities and sororities. Members of clubs may be drawn together by similar goals, such as knitting baby hats for charity or afghans for shelters, or they may be joined by geography or habit, like a lunchtime group that meets at a workplace or school or a whack of knitters that gathers in a community. Usually there are no dues to get in; you can simply infiltrate them with your charm. Bring yarn and brownies. That gets you right into most of them.

A knitting club (like any other club) can be sort of cliquish. If you don't feel as though you fit in and you've given it a fair shake, don't sweat it. Find another one or start your own.

Three Ways
to Start a Knitting Group

1. **Place signs in a yarn shop** telling other knitters what you're up to. (It doesn't hurt to mention that you may have snacks. Snacks are a powerful motivator.)

2. **Stack yarn in separate piles.** The fumes attract other knitters.

3. **Have a goal and tell everyone** you meet about it. Are you going to make bootees for a nearby hospital? Trade stash? Knitters, like everyone else, really like to have a clear mission.

Join Us Wednesdays at 5 pm

Knit & Nibble
for a Notable Cause

Knitting group meets every Wednesday at 5 pm
to knit quick projects for those in need.
We share in providing coffee, tea, and snacks.

Informal Gatherings

These include Stitch n' Bitches, Knit and Natters, Knit Nights, and Sit and Knits. Whatever you call them, they are the frat-party equivalent of Knitting's embassies. They spring up spontaneously in the wild (though some are hosted by yarn shops) and are casual and friendly, usually (much to my delight) have snacks, and sometimes (very much to my delight) have good blender drinks. These gatherings are simply knitters getting together for a good time with no expressed purpose other than the love of a little time to knit. The citizens who attend are diverse and of varying skill, all brought together because they are helpless in the face of wool. The gatherings often breed friendships, spawn obsessions, and support knitters' habits in interesting ways. There are no dues (other than the occasional import of baked goods or tequila, depending on the sort of gathering) and all are welcome. To find them, ask around your yarn community (try yarn shops) or start one yourself.

Etiquette

for Throwing a Perfect Party in Knitting

- Only *white wine, water, and clear soda* may be served. (All other beverages could stain the guests' knitting.)

- *Snack foods* should be served impaled on toothpicks so that knitters' yarn-touching fingers will not be soiled.

- Have *lots of chairs* available.

- Provide *adequate light.* Non-knitter parties are frequently too dark for lace and cable knitters. Candlelight may be flattering, but it isn't going to cut it at a party with a bunch of knitters.

- Provide a *yarn bar.* (A round for all my friends!)

- Offer darning needles and tape measures as *party favors.* (Given the life span of these items, they are ideal gifts.)

- Set up a *trade table.* Knitters bring books, magazines, patterns, and yarn they don't want anymore and put it on the table. At the end of the evening, everyone takes home something he or she does want. (Advise any attending non-knitters or staff not to stand too close to this table; they are likely unprepared for the enthusiasm with which it will be mobbed.)

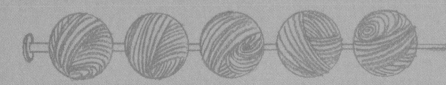

Internet Envoys

One of the big advantages of knitting, I always thought, was that no part of it needed batteries or plugging in or stopped working in a power outage. Knitting (I thought) was something that definitely wasn't going to be improved by technology. Now I think that I was absolutely wrong. The Internet and its instant access to knitters around the world and (believe it or not) the yarn shops of the world means that the entire land of Knitting can be reached through a shiny laptop computer. Lists, groups, blogs, online shops, and e-mail connect us in ways that boggle the mind and astonish me daily. Using your computer this way is easy and fun and makes it a tremendous resource . . . but it does stop working in a power outage.

Lists and Groups

An Internet mailing list or group is a service for knitters (though I hear they have them for other kinds of people too) to communicate with each other worldwide. It's like getting a whole whack of pen pals at the same time. If you search the Web for "knitting groups" or "knitting lists," you'll find hundreds of them. Some of them are about knitting in general (such as the most famous one, the Knitlist, which at the time of this writing has 9,400 subscribers from all over the world). There are lists for sock knitters, ample knitters, charity knitters, slow knitters, knitters with tattoos, male knitters, knitters working on vintage patterns, knitters who use only circular needles, knitters who love cotton, knitters who live in New York City . . . you name it, there's a group out there for your specific interest. When you join a list (there will be instructions for how to do this on a list's Internet page), you can send one e-mail that goes to all of its members at once and you can read the messages of all of the other people on the list. (It's worth noting that when you send an e-mail to a list, it's like standing up in a room full of many, many people. Don't say anything in an e-mail that you wouldn't want to say into the microphone in an auditorium full of that many knitters.)

I've heard people say that knitting friendships that spring up over the Internet are new and radical, but I don't agree. The idea of communicating by letter with a faraway friend (no matter how the letter gets there) is very old-fashioned. Until the advent of e-mail and cheap telephone, this was how friends, lovers, and families stayed in touch. An e-mail just gets there a little faster.

Like any place, Knitting can be reached in many ways. If you haven't found Internet knitters yet, you're missing out. Knitters are everywhere in the virtual world, and unlike backpacking around the world looking for your fellow citizens of Knitting, there you can find your other Knitting travelers easily, quickly, and cheaply. With only your computer and an Internet connection, you can be instantly transported into the lives, living rooms, and yarn shops of knitters all over the world. Wonder what they do about buttonholes in Germany? How about finding out whether Irish knitters really are churning out Arans? The Internet can have you playing virtual show-and-tell with a Norwegian knitter by suppertime.

GATHERING PLACES

CAUTION: The Internet is no place for those who lack will-power. The ability to peer into the yarn shops of the world at 3 a.m. can lead to episodes of extreme yarn commerce. **One minute you're treating insomnia with a little online window shopping at a yarn shop in Denmark, and the next minute you've got two Scandinavian sweater kits in the mail, a dented credit card, and a vaguely dirty feeling.**

PROCEED WITH CAUTION

Five Things
Not to Say to Internet Knitters

1 "My local yarn shop is having a sale." The Internet is a big place. The whole shop will be bought out from under you. If you feel that you simply must pass along sale information, for the love of all things woolly, get your stuff first.

2 The address of your friend Sharon's house (and her phone number for checking the directions). The Internet has as many weirdos as the real world. Don't tell people where you live or reveal too much about yourself or anyone you know. (There is no harm in using a fake name, either.)

3 Anything at all, even if it' s very nice, in all capital letters. TYPING WITH ALL CAPITALS IS INTERNET YELLING. Don't do it, even for emphasis, unless you want it understood that you mean to be screeching at the top of your voice.

4 "The yarn/needles/stitch/fiber that you like is stupid."

5 Anything that you would never, ever say in a yarn shop or a living room. The Internet may be a virtual place, but it is full of real people and the rules for how we interact with each other don't change (no matter how anyone else is behaving) just because we are online.

The KnitList Connection

When I was a young mother at home with three small children, I found myself with two things I wasn't expecting: time to knit and nobody to talk to. There were other things that surprised me, like how much laundry there was, how many washings it takes to get apple juice off the kitchen floor, and how long I could go without a shower if the kids had chicken pox, but the knitting and the lack of talking were the biggest surprises. (To this day, I think these were maybe the biggest adjustments, because knitting and talking are basically my only two activities.) Sure, I could talk to the kids, but they were little and read so few novels that our conversations rarely made it past whether I had sliced their oranges in a manner that was acceptable to them — and despite all of my efforts, they really couldn't have conversations about knitting.

I tried joining a mothers group in my neighborhood. The contact with other mothers was wonderful, and I still use the muffin recipe I learned that summer, but all we talked about was our kids and how to do a good job of raising them. (I was briefly bitter that this was the case, but then I realized that you can't be bitter about joining a mothering group and finding the members interested only in mothering.) I longed for contact that had a whole string of discourse unrelated to getting babies' spit-up off your last clean T-shirt or learning the best time-out place for a toddler. I wanted — dare I dream it — an exchange with another breathing human that didn't contain the word *poo-poo*. It was elusive. I knit alone. I needed to find other knitters.

One evening, a geeky friend came over and suggested that I use our family computer for something other than collecting dust and playing solitaire. He proposed that I do a search for something I thought was interesting. I have a somewhat narrow focus, so I typed "knitting" and found a mailing list called the Knitlist. I didn't know it at the time, but I was saved and my whole life was about to change.

The Knitlist put me in touch with thousands of other knitters all over the world. You could write in and ask how to make buttonholes or why cotton stretched out of shape or answer a question about mohair. Nobody flinched when you said that the new needles from Patons made you dizzy with glee and everyone understood when a knitter wrote in exhausted and staggering from another battle in the gauge wars. Remarkably, after being a solitary knitter for the whole first part of my life, right out of the blue I'd found my people. The online knitters led me to local knitters, the mailing list led me to personal Web sites and blogs. I met knitters who have gone on to be wonderful mentors, casual accomplices, and treasured friends. The Knitlist did for me what any good embassy or consulate does for stray or lonely citizens: It connected me to my compatriots and showed me the doors to gathering places. In my case, it started with the Knitlist. For you, it could be anywhere.

Knitting Blogs

A blog (short for Web log) is a Web-based log of what's going on in a knitter's life. (I hear there are blogs for other topics such as politics and cooking, but I've never looked at them.) A blog is sort of like a virtual living room. Usually, a blogger (someone who blogs) writes about her knitting, yarn, fibers, adventures, and disasters and publishes it with pictures on her Web page. A blog is different from a regular Internet site in two ways: First, it is simple to make and use so it can be changed and updated every day (or every hour, should your knitting angst demand it). Second, it is usually interactive. Customarily, a blog has a spot where you can add your comments on the topic of the day and read the comments of others. This means that blogs often very quickly become communities of like-minded yarn-loving friends. I have a blog at www.yarnharlot.com, and it's proved a lovely spot both to play show-and-tell and to meet knitty friends.

Has Your Online Yarn Shopping Gone Too Far? Maybe, If . . .

- **You now get so many packages** of yarn in the mail that you are starting to think about knitting the letter carrier some socks just to make the guilt go away.

- **The last time you had to enter a credit card** number, you realized that you have it (along with the card's expiration date) completely memorized.

- **A package of yarn has arrived** (and it's a pretty big one) and you have no memory of ordering it.

Some Knitters Are an Island

Some knitters aren't looking for knitting friends. For some knitters, knitting is their friend (sort of; it's not like they don't have human friends too). Knitting is a force that brings them back into themselves, a private intention, a discreet diversion. These knitters inhabit the natural flip side to the social knitters scene, and they are wonderful surprises along the knitter's path. To discover that someone you thought was an ordinary person is actually a knitter: It's like kicking rocks with your shoe and discovering a diamond.

From: alicek@snegt.knit
Subject: Yarn Fumes
Date: October 18
To: kmarg@symport.knit
Subject: Yarn Fumes?

So last night I'm in the yarn shop. (Stop that. I only went for a darning needle. I lost another one — I swear they must get sucked into the same black hole that consumes tape measures. And before you judge me for being in the yarn shop for the second time this week, the new sock yarn you were interested in has arrived. You might want to hustle; it's going fast.) I saw a new knitting book and flipped through it in a relaxed way. I thought it was beautiful, but not really my style. Then I went over to the laceweight for a while and I thought about making a shawl. (Who am I kidding? I'm really not ready for knitting with something that's got the same thickness as dental floss.) Then I hung out with some mohair — you know, the one that everybody's been knitting up into that jacket. (I'm still not sure about that jacket. Wouldn't the mohair get stuck all over your clothes? I really think being covered in cat hair might be enough of a fashion statement for me.) Then I chatted with Leah for a bit and left.

Now, I swear to you that I'd made an intelligent and carefully reasoned decision not to buy anything. I'd gone to the yarn store for a darning needle and damn it, that's what I was going to leave with. I've got tons of projects on the needles and I promised myself that the stash wasn't going to outgrow the box in the hall closet. But here's the thing: I got back to the car after saying goodbye to Leah and I put my store bag on the seat beside me. That's when I noticed that it was a little big . . . huge, in fact. Leah had given me a suspiciously large bag, considering that I bought only a packet of darning needles.

I opened the bag and peeked in, and frankly, I was stunned . . . completely stunned. Inside the bag was that new knitting book that I didn't really care for, some of the laceweight I decided was beyond me, a whole stinking kit for the mohair jacket that's probably going to shed more than the cat does . . . and I don't really recall buying any of it. You guys talk about "accidental" yarn purchases all the time, but this is the first time it's ever happened to me. I went in there to buy a darning needle. Really. I was so stunned that I checked the receipt. My signature was on the credit card slip.

Yarn Fumes. That's got to be what it is. You walk into the shop and all of that fiber is off-gassing yarn fumes, which totally influence the part of your brain responsible for impulsive behavior. It's either this explanation (and I think we really should consider it) or Leah's taken to subtle oxygen deprivation to make us more vulnerable while we're in the store. Of course, it's not enough to injure anyone — just enough so that you end up with a whole whack of yarn you weren't expecting to own.

Either way, I'm wearing a gas mask the next time I need a darning needle.

Alice

(P.S. Think carefully before you mock me. In the bag there was also some of that sock yarn you want.)

Five Ways
to Scope Out a New Yarn Shop

Do not think for even one moment that yarn shops do not have your number. The owners may be your friends. They may even feel like the only people who really understand you. But remember: They are also the people who ordered all of that Australian merino on which you just blew your budget. Trust no one and use these survival tips.

1. **New yarn shops** can be overwhelming. There is a great deal of new stuff there to absorb. Take deep breaths and try to get your bearings.

2. **Establish the boundaries** of the store and keep the exit in sight.

3. **Keep your hands** in your pockets for at least ten minutes. Touching the yarn is what puts most knitters over the top. Just look, do not touch. If a yarn shop employee approaches you straight away, tell her you are just looking; you can get help later when you are less stunned and vulnerable. Don't let her hand you anything. That's touching.

4. **Do NOT linger** at the cash register. Get out your money before you approach it and keep your eyes looking straight ahead.

5. **Observe the twenty-minute rule.** You must want something (without being distracted, coveting something else, or picking up other yarn) for twenty consecutive minutes. If you still want it, it's fair game.

From: kmarg@symport.knit

To: tipplor@coolmail.knit

Date October 18

Subject: Another one bites the dust

Tasha,

I just got an e-mail from Alice. Man, she cracks me up. She had her first out-of-body yarn shop experience and she's a little tripped because she ended up in the car with yarn and doesn't really remember buying it. I'm thinking about writing her back and telling her how normal that is. I don't remember buying half of the stash.

I had to laugh, too, because she's still holding on to the cute idea that her stash will always fit in that one box in the closet. Remember when you thought it would always fit in that trunk in your living room? Good times.

Margaret

(P.S. She says that new sock yarn is in.)

Five Ways
to Leave a Yarn Shop
without Spending Any Money

IMPORTANT NOTE: This strategy has never been adequately proved. Knitters have left with some money and knitters have left with more money than they expected, but I know of only three knitters who have ever left a yarn shop without spending a dime. The first was broke and had no money to spend; the second was coming down with the flu; and the third was a knitter of considerable experience, stash, and immunity. Do not attempt this stunt too far from payday. You can't eat cashmere.

1. **Just as with the grocery store,** don't go in hungry. Hang out with your stash before you go. Give your best stuff a little squeeze, maybe place a little silk in your purse in case you start feeling as though you don't own anything good. This is yarn's first trick: making you think all your other yarn sucks.

2. **Don't go in frustrated.** Going in when your arse is being kicked by a vicious project is like staggering into a cool desert oasis after struggling through the Sahara without water for four days. (Yarn trick #2: Anything is possible when you are in a yarn shop.)

3. **Do not take your debit card** or checkbook. Bring only cash. Spending it hurts a little more and helps keep it real.

4 **Do not linger at the cash register.** This is where they put all the good stuff. Those tiny little skeins? Don't touch them; they're cashmere. Yarn shops are clever enough to put anything that's a seductive little impulse buy right there where you have to wait.

5 **Do not engage in conversation.** "Have you seen the new sock book?" may seem invitational and kind and helpful, but it's just a scam. Stay alert.

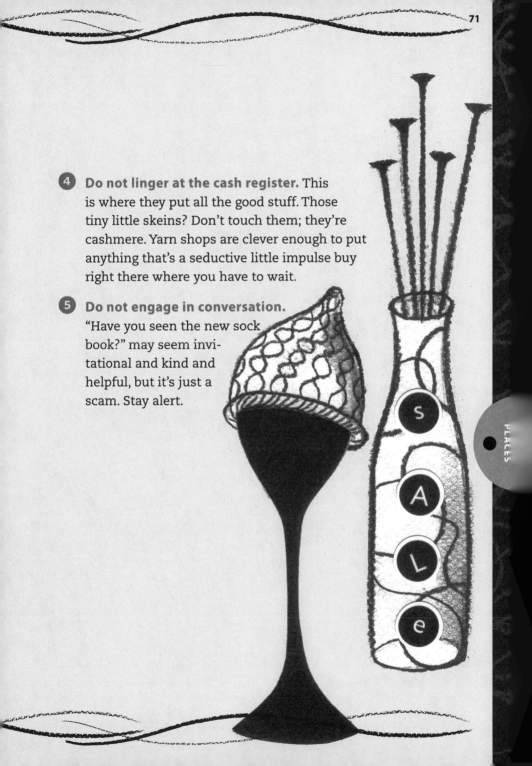

November 7

Dear Meg,

I'm certain that as the owner of our local yarn shop, you will have received requests like this before, and I hope that you do not judge me too harshly. I love my wife more than I can tell you and her happiness means the world to me, so it is with a heavy heart that I make this request. Please stop selling her yarn. Or don't sell her so much . . . or something. I'm desperate. The apartment is full, the car is full, the freezer is full, and there's yarn down the sleeves of all the coats we're not wearing. There's so much yarn that I don't even think she knows what she has anymore, and that's a shame, because I remember how much she loved some of the yarn that she's totally buried now.

I know it sounds like I'm a little bit selfish, and maybe I am, but I really do miss being able to see out of the bedroom windows, and I think that Alice does too because she's spoken several times about "getting the yarn under control." (I'm not sure what that means, but it seems it would be easier if she knit up some of what she has.)

For the record, I don't think her behavior is crazy or anything. I know that she's just collecting what she needs to work in her chosen art form. I just think maybe her eyes are bigger than her ~~stomach~~ knitting needles right now.

Sincerely,

Andy Price

(P.S. I don't see any reason to tell Alice I sent this letter.)

Five Ways
to Determine That You Need
to Find a New Yarn Shop

1 No yarn.

2 Lots of yarn, but none of it matches. (Single-ball syndrome is horrible.)

3 When your buddy drops a stitch, someone yells, "Dumbass!"

4 You see something fluttering over by the Shetland wool.

5 Every time you ask a question, one of the staff says, "Look it up."

Useful Translation

Do you have this in blue?
I was thinking that I would like to make a blue sweater. If you don't have this in blue, I'm probably not leaving here without some yarn anyway. Oh, is that red?

HISTORY OF THIS LAND:
HOW DID KNITTING GET HERE?

IF YOU'RE REALLY GOING TO understand a place and a culture, then it goes without saying that you need to know a little of its history. Many knitters, myself included, enjoy not just the act of knitting, but also the act of connection with so many who have knit before us. Knitting is a simple thing; the history of knitting is not anything like the history of transportation, which involves the invention of the wheel, the combustion engine, and the airplane. On the day of its conception, knitting involved just one knitter with sticks and some string doing almost exactly what you and I are doing today, only with different yarn, needles, and swear words.

In his wonderful book *The History of Handknitting,* Richard Rutt tells us that the earliest surviving piece of knitted fabric was discovered in Islamic Egypt and probably dates from sometime around 1000 CE. If that seems vague, it's because it is, partly due to the fragile nature of knitted objects (yarn just doesn't hold up over the course of hundreds of years the way we would all hope) and partly because no one realized what was happening at the time. It's not as though someone looked over at the first knitter, saw what she was doing, and said, "Wow, did you just think that up, because man, I think this is going to really catch on. Wait — let me get a tablet and carve your name in it. This is really historic."

In fact, we don't know exactly who the first knitter even was — a tragic loss for all of us. It isn't like the invention of the telephone or the iron, which was instantly recognized as useful to humanity, and nobody ever filed a patent for the first sock. Because this wonder occurred in anonymity, the facts about the first knitter are pretty loose, which reduces me to making educated guesses about the life of the person who gave us the world of knitting based on what little evidence there is.

The first knitter probably lived in Egypt sometime between 1000 and 1500 CE, and we guess that it was a woman, given that women did most of the handwork at that time. It's possible it was a man, however; the craft may have been invented by nomadic Arabs who spread the idea as they traveled. If this is the case, then knitting may have been invented by a shepherd, bored out of his stinking gourd as he watched his flocks. This first knitter was also likely a spinner, or lived with one, because there were no yarn shops. She or he was likely Muslim and probably did *nalbinding* — that is, created a fabric that looks a lot like knitting, except that it's done with a needle and thread. At it's simplest, it consists of rounds of loops, just like circular knitting, except these loops aren't kept live on the needles. Each round of loops forms intact fabric, like in crochet, and the nalbinder goes around and around, sewing more loops into the ones below it, creating whatever shape and size she wants. This explanation makes it sound easy, but as with knitting, the size and shape of what you end up with has a lot to do with luck and skill. In addition, the nalbinder must rethread the needle with yarn each time the length is used up. When I imagine nalbinding an entire pair of socks and how many times the worker has to rethread her needle, I figure that knitting had to be invented to avoid weaving in all those ends.

The First Sock

I wish I'd known the first knitter. I really do. I want to know what she was thinking. How did she figure it out? How on earth did she ever think, "You know, if I had some sticks, I bet I could loop this string and make clothes faster than the way I'm doing it now." The oldest surviving piece of knitting is a sock, knit in the round at a simply staggering gauge of thirty-six stitches to the inch, and most of the other early examples are more of the same, sometimes with Arabic patterns knit in. We don't know if this means that the first item ever knit was a sock, but it puts the chances right up there. (There is pretty much no evidence that the first thing ever knit was a long winter scarf, something that modern-day knitters will find quite difficult to imagine.) In light of the fact that we twenty-first-century knitters consider socks a pretty advanced trick for knitters and that few of us would advocate that a beginner start with a sock straight out of the gate, we should all be blown away that this first knitter, the one who invented the act, probably made a sock. And because circular needles are a more modern invention, she knit this first sock in the round on whatever were the medieval equivalent of double-pointed needles (probably wire sharpened on a stone). She turned a heel, she fashioned a toe — and she did it all by herself, without benefit of a yarn shop, a knitting teacher, knitting friends, a book, the Internet, or even a sympathetic fellow knitter. She simply sat down and pulled this idea out of the ether. I can hardly tell you how much this moves me.

There are really two ways to go about knitting a sock. You can either start at the cuff and work downward to the toe or you can begin at the toe and head up. I've always resisted the "toe-up" sock, subscribing to the notion (I'm a little stuck in my ways) that knitting it "cuff down" is more traditional and old-fashioned. This method made me feel connected with the older ways of doing things, made me feel as though the first knitter was resonating within me.

Imagine my shock when I learned that the first socks ever knit on this planet were probably knit "toe up." My whole world shifted.

Knitting's Beginnings

When exactly was that moment when the first knitter, the human to whom we owe all of our knitting hours, while making a pair of socks to keep her family warm, threaded her nalbinding needle for the 456th time, sighed deeply, and thought, "Holy crap. There has got to be a better way"?

Considering how smart knitting makes me feel, I bet she experienced a moment of high self-esteem. It's too bad she isn't around to see what happened after that moment, the way knitting took off from there. I find it incredibly profound that now, seven hundred years later, as I sit in my living room knitting a pair of socks for my own child, I am doing something almost exactly as the first knitter did it. The construction of a sock has changed very little (human feet have changed even less) and the act of forming a stitch in knitting hasn't changed at all. First Knitter sat there and did as I do now: She put the needle into the stitch, she wrapped her yarn around, she pulled the needle back through, she slipped her new stitch from one needle to the other, and she marveled at her cleverness at making something out of nothing.

I also imagine that she wondered if she was ever going to finish the pair before her kid outgrew them . . . and that's another thing we have in common.

Where's the Crap?

One very interesting thing about early knitting is that — and I cannot stress this enough — none of it sucks. It is all knitted at a gauge that most knitters today would absolutely refuse to entertain, and it is frequently worked using brilliant Fair Isle technique and intarsia that would stun even a modern master knitter into breathless respect. Nobody has ever found a practice piece, a sock that wouldn't go on a foot, or even a swatch.

How is this possible, when your house (and mine) is littered with knitting disasters? Some possible explanations:

• They were smarter than we are.

• Part of the tradition of the ancient knitter's culture was to burn your knitting in a fit of rage if it didn't work out. (If this is the case, it's a shame that we let the tradition go. I bet it's pretty cathartic.)

- **They treasured** only the good stuff well enough that it was preserved.
- **They held themselves to** an ancient standard of excellence that we can never hope to achieve.
- **Moths have done** them a really big favor.

Five Things
about Knitting That
the First Knitter and I Have in Common

1 At best, she knew two stitches, knit and purl, just like me. Everything knit from the moment First Knitter thought of the act until I started with it has still been made from only these two stitches or a combination of them.

2 Even though there are only two stitches, I bet she realized and I know I realize that there is still a seemingly inexhaustible number of ways to arse them up.

3 I bet First Knitter didn't have enough yarn storage space either — or her sheep were crowded.

4 I bet that at least once, when her children or her goats or another woman who wanted her to walk to the Nile on a water run came in while she was knitting, she lifted her head and said, "Just one more row."

5 I bet First Knitter's first socks didn't fit her either. (I'm actually willing to take bets that, just like my first socks, they didn't fit anybody.)

Notable Dates in Knitting History

AROUND 1000 CE: Knitting was invented, or, more appropriately, it evolved from other crafts that were similar. Nobody is absolutely positive, but I'm pretty sure that the first knitter was pretty freaking pleased with herself and, aside from being the first person to knit, was the first person to wake up a member of her family to show them what she'd done with sticks and string. Not coincidentally, the first knitter was probably also the first person to realize that non-knitters really don't want to talk about it. This must have been a crushing blow, considering that for the inventor, every single person in the entire rest of the world was a non-knitter.

1000: The first knitter likely realized that she didn't have enough matching yarn for her father's socks and invented the stripe so nobody could tell she failed to plan ahead. A thousand years later, those of us who are still failing to plan ahead are quite grateful.

1500: Big changes. The purl stitch arrived on the scene, used mostly for decorative patterns. It's my opinion that purl stitches

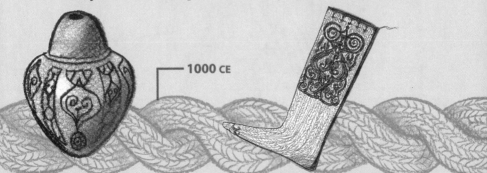

1000 CE

HISTORY

were probably invented long before this, but someone always "corrected" the knitter.

1525: A knitter ran out of lamp oil at 8:30 the night before her daughter's birthday and invented the Stitch n' Bitch when she went to the house next door, where another knitter still had the lights on. (I'm guessing on this one, but it seems likely.)

1527: The first knitting guild was formed in Paris. Only men were admitted and it took six years for students to become full-fledged master knitters.

1527: Right after the guild was invented, I imagine that a fair number of women got right ticked that men had found another way to have more jobs and money than they were allowed to have.

1571: A statute called An Act for the Continuance of the Making of Caps was passed in England in an attempt to give the cap-knitting industry a boost. It made law that every person at

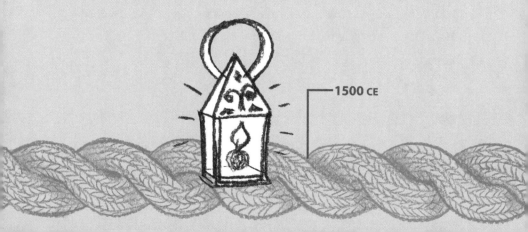

1500 CE

least six years old had to wear a cap knit in England on all of the Sabbath and holy days. While I think this is a pretty good way to force people to buy, use, and appreciate knitting, it apparently didn't catch on and the act was repealed in 1597.

1589: The Reverend William Lee invented the first knitting machine in England. Rumor has it that he did so to give his wife more free time to pander to him, but I'm giving him the benefit of the doubt and assuming he was just really interested in the art. In any case, when he went to Queen Elizabeth for a patent, she refused, claiming that she didn't want to put hand-knitters out of work. Lee's invention wasn't given a patent until after he (and the queen) died, when his brother obtained one.

1590–1594: Shakespeare wrote *Two Gentlemen of Verona* and in it one of his characters lists the virtues of the woman he loves: She can sew, brew good ale, milk, spin, and . . . knit him a stocking. This proves two things: By 1590, knitting was well known enough to be mentioned in pop culture, and knitters had already figured out that hand-knit socks were a magical key to a lover's heart.

HISTORY

1590 CE

1700–1750: A knitter in the Netherlands created an incredible petticoat now in the collection of the Victoria and Albert Museum. It's knit out of very fine two-ply wool and measures 2½ feet by 10 feet, and the whole surface of the petticoat uses purl stitches to illustrate flowers, vines, elephants, lions, birds, rhinoceroses, ostriches, and other animals. The patterns are complicated and intricate, and, most unbelievably, do not repeat over the entire 10-foot surface. Nobody knows the name of the knitter and, more important, nobody knows if she or he was at all sane upon finishing.

1840: Shetland lace knitting, incredibly delicate and complex, developed in the Shetland Islands. In a remarkably quick period of time, knitters were turning out whole shawls so light and fine that the entire length of them could be drawn through a wedding ring. (They didn't go looking for the guy in the village with the biggest hands to test them, either.)

1854 (OR SO): The Earl of Raglan had an arm amputated after a battle in the Crimean War. His tailor (clearly a smart guy) invented the diagonal shoulder seam to make it easier for the earl to dress himself. We can only imagine how ticked off the tailor would be to know that all of these years later we're knitting a sweater named for the wearer instead of the brilliant inventor.

Circa1854 CE

1857: The Seventh Earl of Cardigan (who led the charge of the Light Brigade) had a reputation for being a questionable commander but a seriously sharp dresser, and when he took command of his regiment, he used his fortune to make them the best-dressed force around. (It did not help.) The soldiers wore woolen button-front jackets, which have come, of course, to be called *cardigans*.

1860: The Samurai warriors of Japan found themselves unemployed and took up knitting to supplement their income. They made socks and gloves of exquisite fineness. This didn't last long, though, and the warriors-turned-knitters became obsolete with the arrival of the Industrial Revolution and knitting machines.

1875: West of Portugal, in the Azores Islands, knitters began making very fine pieces of lace not out of wool or silk, but from the fiber of the Azores cactus plant seed. While their work was remarkable, the question still remains: How exactly did these knitters figure out that they could make doilies from a cactus?

1860 CE

HISTORY

1900: Dentdale, England, became known for its knitters. They were very fast and productive and churned out knitwear to supplement their families' incomes. They knit in church (for which they were reportedly rebuked by the pastor . . . but they didn't stop) and knit together in the evenings to save on light and heat. Called the Terrible Knitters of Dent (with *terrible* being used exactly the way a teenager would use *wicked* these days), these knitters have become a vivid part of Dentdale's history.

1917: During World War I, every woman, boy, girl, and man who was injured or unfit for duty in Canada, the United States, and Britain was implored to knit for soldiers. Children knit in schools; men and women knit on the streets and in groups in the evenings. The need for socks was so great that in one instance, if anyone had any wool she hadn't turned into a pair of socks within twenty-one days, she was asked to turn it in for use by another, faster knitter. (Clearly, the idea of a closeted, secret stash was out of the question.)

1917 CE

1921: His Royal Highness Edward VIII, Prince of Wales, took a fancy to wearing intricate Fair Isle sweaters and set off a fashion trend that had everyone wearing them all through the 1920s. His fondness for the colorwork sweaters sparked the commercialization of sweater production in the Shetland Islands. Unless you are from the Shetland Islands, you probably know about these sweaters because he wore them. Reportedly, the king-to-be was a knitter, though it is not known whether he ever knit for Wallis Simpson, the woman for whom he abdicated the throne.

1939: The depression in Sweden was terrible, and out of desperation (and some clever thinking), Bohus Stickning (meaning Bohus Knitting) was born. The group, largely the brainchild of Emma Jacobsson, was a home-based knitting co-op to help women earn extra money for their families. The group quickly developed intricate colorwork patterns that included Fair Isle–style work with both knit and purl stitches in the patterning. These sweaters became truly popular and many were exported all over the world. Economics improved in the 1960s and Bohus Stickning closed shop in 1969.

1921 CE

1953: The first commercial polyester fiber was put into production by the Dupont company. With this invention began a knitterly debate, raging to this day, over its role in knitting.

1954: A knitter used a synthetic yarn for the first time and didn't care for it at all. In her firm conviction on this topic, she stated in public that she would never use it again. Another knitter overheard her and took it personally (because at that moment she had on the needles a scarf of that very yarn) and in two seconds of heated foolishness there occurred the first recorded use of the term *yarn snob*. It has stuck.

1958: Elizabeth Zimmermann became modern knitting's first foreign service operative when she published the first issue of her newsletter, "Wool Gathering." From there she went on to lead a remarkable life, punctuated entirely by her love of knitting and her knack for spreading the word and teaching knitters how to think.

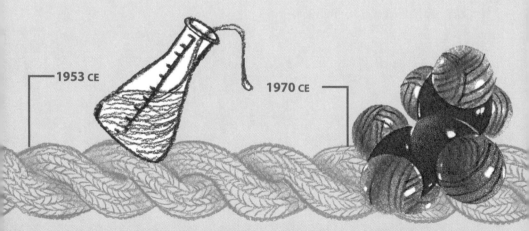

1953 CE

1970 CE

1970s: Acrylic yarn became very popular as knitters were rapidly overwhelmed by the cool idea of never hand-washing anything again. Sadly, much of the acrylic yarn from this period was scratchy and stiff and didn't breathe, and many children were imprisoned in furnace-impersonating sweaters for decades before acrylics improved. (We shall not discuss Phentex slippers.)

1984: I was totally screwed over by my first adult-size sweater, which, owing to a bit of trouble involving gauge, would have fit an adult elephant. I neither learned my lesson nor was put off, and knit several more monstrosities before catching on at all.

Useful Translation

Would you like this yarn?

I hate this yarn. I wouldn't ever have bought it, but it was 50 percent off. I swear I have no ability to discriminate when yarn is half price. You should see me if it's 60 percent off. I'll buy anything. It turns out that there is no such thing as bad yarn . . . you just have to find every knitter's magic price. Now that I'm away from the sale-yarn fumes and I'm coming to my senses, I'm realizing that this yarn is pretty freaking ugly and I'm trying to pass it off to you. Please fall for it.

GEOGRAPHY

BECAUSE KNITTING HAS SUCH WILD and loose borders, and because those borders move all the time as people
take up residence in the country, there is little that can be said
about the geography of the greater land of Knitting. We can say
there are mountains, for Peruvian knitters high in the Andes are
making caps right now. We can say there are oceans, because
knitters in the British Isles make fishermen sweaters. In fact, all
over the globe, knitters are busy churning out a variety of objects that would stagger the imagination. Instead, we turn to the
more personal geography of Knitting. You may find Knitting's
geography all over the planet, but some geography you can find
only in Knitting. Of all of these features, the most significant is
the phenomenon of *stash*.

Stash may be found wherever you find a knitter. These geo-
graphic formations vary a great deal from knitter to knitter and
their evolution follows that of the knitters in the area. Naturally
formed stashes often reflect an area's influences. For example,
a wild stash that has sprung up in an area near a great many
sheep farms may be quite wool-heavy, while an urban stash
zone may contain fibers from several contributing yarn shops
that empty into the area. Young stashes are often quite small,
containing little yarn and often fitting into small areas such as
boxes and bags in closets; mature stashes may have overrun
much of an entire building.

Mature stashes are in fact extremely invasive and oppor-
tunistic and very often grow *stashlets,* which are offshoots of
the parent stash. These stashlets are often located in surprising places such as freezers, kitchen drawers, and boxes shoved
under beds. Knitters who live with large stashes and stashlets
are frequently surprised to discover fiber that they don't recall
contributing. There is some evidence that stashes breed or influence a knitter to procure more fiber against her will. Aggressive
stashes may exert an almost psychic control over their knitters,
encouraging them to obtain more and more yarn for them and
overrunning all available storage space. Stashes can become
wild if they're not properly managed, and some knitters have
even been attacked by these feral types, with skeins and balls of
yarn leaping on them in an attempt to gain attention (or escape)
when the knitters open a closet containing them.

Geographical Peril: Stash Overload

"He who would travel happily must travel light."

— **Antoine de Saint-Exupéry**

How much stash, exactly, is too much stash? I've spent years and years advocating a stash of whatever size pleases you, and I still do. There's very little I can think of that can give a knitter more satisfaction and inspiration (and can guard against more emergencies) than a large stash. It's like a personalized yarn shop right in your house. (That's a goal, not a problem.) There's another side to a huge stash, though. Besides the obvious dangers (suffocation, complete lack of closet space), a stash that grows out of control can have the opposite effect, eventually burdening the knitter with the weight of unrealized hopes and dreams. A stash full of opportunity and hope is one thing; it's another when a collection is so large that the beautiful things you once had fond hopes for are now hopelessly buried.

The optimum size for a stash is dictated by a number of factors: personality, family tolerance, budget, and storage space. This is how two knitters, one with hundreds and hundreds of skeins of yarn and one with twenty, can each tell you with complete honesty that she has "tons of yarn."

Super sweet STASH! 2³⁹ LB.

Phases of Stashing

Anyone who has read the famous work of Dr. Elisabeth Kübler-Ross can tell you that she defined the five stages of grief: denial, anger, bargaining, depression, and acceptance. I've often noticed that these phases apply to a lot more than grief. I once had a car that died in these five stages. ("Bargaining" resulted in the car running only on premium gas and not stalling as long as I never made a right turn.) I was not surprised, then, to discover that the birth and development of a stash follow these same phases.

DENIAL: The knitter, being too young, too broke, or too uninvolved, has no stash. She purchases yarn for each individual project on an "as-needed" basis and feels somewhat befuddled and confused by and superior to knitters who have an extensive stash. After all, this knitter has no need to hoard wool like some kind of justice-driven sheep. It's all about control. This knitter believes she has no stash because she is in control.

ANGER: Although there is now quite a bit of yarn in the house, the knitter reacts angrily to any insinuation that it is a stash. She insists that all of this yarn is just the leftovers from the last project and some stuff that's going to be the next project or two. She resents the insinuation that the yarn collection isn't completely controlled. She talks about how she's going to make a hat with the leftovers and a sweater with the bag of yarn that she just bought and there isn't going to be a stash. It's just planning ahead and that's not a stash.

BARGAINING: The knitter has continued to plan ahead by buying yarn for the next two (or twenty) projects that she is going to undertake, but the stash has made a critical leap. The knitter now purchases yarn that has no purpose at all, perhaps because it's on sale, perhaps because she saw it as a unique opportunity, perhaps because it was discontinued. The knitter is buying yarn more freely now, but the process is marked by bargaining: "I'll buy the blue merino, but I won't start working with it until I finish the green shawl"; "I'm going to buy only as much yarn as will fit in the hall closet"; or "I'll buy yarn, but only sale yarn or really good yarn or yarn that I really need."

ACCEPTANCE: The stash now has a mind of its own and the knitter is its loyal handmaiden. It grows according to its own whims and although the knitter may speak sometimes about "getting the stash under control" or the admittedly vague "doing something about the stash," she doesn't stop obtaining yarn and she doesn't really mean to. Because she has fully accepted the stash, when she says "I'll do something about the stash," she's talking not about getting rid of the yarn, but of buying under-bed storage so it stops falling out of the overfull hall closet. The knitter and the yarn have attained a symbiotic relationship. They need each other.

DEATH: Because part of the acceptance phase usually involves a knitter becoming SABLE (Stash Acquisitive Beyond Life Expectancy), a stash usually outlives the knitter, becoming a kind of woolen legacy that does not die, but instead moves on to new knitters.

Because
stashes never die,
knitters live on too.
It's almost poetic.

Five Ways
You Can Tell
That Your Stash Has Gone Too Far

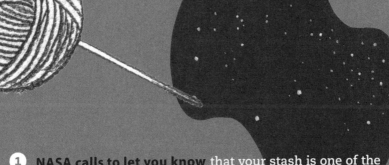

1. **NASA calls to let you know** that your stash is one of the objects visible from space, like the Great Wall of China or the pyramids.

2. **Your local yarn shop calls to see** if you have any more of the blue merino.

3. **One of your kids crank-calls** you to tell you that your stash is larger than allowed by law, and before you recognize his voice, you believe him.

4. **You go to the sock-yarn sale** and realize that the selection in your bedroom closet is really much better.

5. **Sometimes, every once in a long while** and only at night, you are a little bit afraid.

ENVIRONMENTAL ISSUES

UNLIKE PEST OR WEED CONTROL, there has been little research into stash control, or, at least, little has been done by knitters to research stash-control methods that may reduce the stash conception rate. (It's possible that much research has been entertained by those who live with knitters and are trying to get back enough closet space to hang up their shirts, but knitters haven't been paying much attention to these people and their problems.)

Most knitters have discovered that stashes are like gardens: They decrease in size only when the environment demands it and their owners run out of seed money or space. While well-established stashes are very difficult to eliminate, they can be weeded and reined in enough for knitters to obtain some measure of control again.

How to Weed a Stash

1 **If your stash has grown to occupy several areas, consolidate it.** It is somewhat normal to need to move some furniture to accomplish this and it's a good idea to begin the process when you don't expect other members of the family to be home for some time. Remember not to block your exits.

2 **Survey the stash and begin sorting.** I stash sort by yarn type, making piles of lace yarn, sock yarn, worsted, and so forth. If I come across any yarn that was purchased in quantity for projects (an entire sweater's worth, for example), I put that together and make a projects pile.

3 **Once you have it all organized, start thinking about what is obviously not useful to you any longer.** Has it been ten years since you knit with acrylic? It can probably go. Is there anything you really don't like? (There's no reason to wonder what you're doing with yarn you don't like. We all understand yarn-shop accidents.) Start pulling out anything that's a bad color, a weight you haven't knit since you were learning, or bought only because it was on sale at 50 percent off. (Nobody can resist such a sale. You're only human.)

4 Place into an opaque garbage bag anything that you pull out of the stash. Do not use a clear bag or a box; either makes it too easy to get sentimental over what you're pitching. Put it into the bag and don't look back.

5 Get honest. Are you really ever going to knit that sweet little sweater with the cowboy on the front? I know it made sense when you bought the kit, but if the son you were going to make if for graduated from college last year, put it in the bag. Are there thirty balls of mohair even though you know knitting mohair makes you sneeze? What about that sequined novelty yarn you bought before you realized that you're never going back to a disco? Did you once love chunky jackets and now knit only lace? Why would you need sock yarn if you know you don't knit socks? Look at the stash with a critical eye, accept your growth and change as a knitter, and put into the bag anything that you've outgrown. Be brutal. Remember that you are freeing up psychic (and literal) space for yarn you love.

6 If at any point you falter, feel dizzy, find yourself panicking, or discover that you're taking items back out of the bag, repeat the stash weeder's mantra: I am a knitter of discerning taste. Yarn is meant to have a future, and yarn I don't love won't ever be knit. I am not getting rid of yarn; I am liberating it that it may achieve its full potential with another knitter.

Where to Take the Bag When You're Done

- **Donate it to Goodwill** or another place that raises cash for charity by selling old stuff.
- **Sell the contents** in a garage sale. (But don't do this unless you are absolutely positive you have the willpower to watch people take away your yarn without calling it all back again. This method is not for knitters with separation issues.)
- **A local retirement home** probably would love to have it.
- **Schools often want yarn** for arts and crafts projects.
- **Knitters who knit for charity** really appreciate donations of yarn. Ask around your yarn shop and see who would like to have it for charity projects.

November 27

Grace,

I know that you're probably pretty sick of hearing about the knitting, but after learning about that horrible date you had last week, I had to tell you about a woman I met at knitting group. Her name is Sue and she's got a hysterical method for screening dates: She goes out with them and smiles and chats and gets to know them, and then at some point during the evening, she reaches into her purse and pulls out her knitting. She can knit while she's talking, and she chooses something really simple so that she doesn't have to look at her work . . . and then she knits, right there in the bar or restaurant — no explanation, no "do you mind if I knit." She says nothing, not one word. She knits merrily along, continuing to chat and smile . . . and she waits. His reaction helps her decide if he gets a second date. Some guys are stunned and can hardly talk anymore. They keep breaking off mid-sentence and staring at her hands, trying to figure out what's going on. These guys re not going to make the cut. (Clearly, they have no communication skills.)

Some guys ask what she's making and why she's doing it, and as long as they express positive interest, then they're probably going to get a second date. (One date, however, asked, "And how long have you been like this?" which is hardly positive; it makes knitting sound like a weird deformity or disease.)

When she brings out the knitting, once in a while a guy shifts uncomfortably in his seat and looks around desperately to see who's staring at them. This guy may even go so far as to ask her to stop or to say, "Are you really going to do that here?" His face grows red, he loosens his tie, and he can't stop watching the door to make sure that nobody he knows comes in and catches him with the weird knitting chic. No second date for this kind, and as a matter of fact, Sue says that any guy who asks her to stop knitting during dinner is lucky she doesn't excuse herself to go to the bathroom so she can slip out a window into the night, trailing yarn as she goes.

Sue dreams of a gentleman who says he finds her knitting thrilling, that he's never known a woman as clever as she, and that asks if she'll show him how this enchanting thing is done because he's always wondered . . .

The Holy Grail, though, the man whom Sue is waiting for, her knight in shining armor, her paramour for life and the shepherd of her heart, will be the man who looks at her with warm affection and tender joy, is polite and kind and funny and brave, and, when Sue pulls out her knitting on that first date, smiles at her with surprised delight and says, "I can't believe I've found you," while reaching into his bag for his fine merino sweater in progress.

What a great system.

Love,
Alice

Lose Two Turns

INTERESTING SIGHTS:
THE BLACK HOLE

EVERY KNITTER HAS A CONNECTION with the arcane experience of a black hole. Although black holes are rare in the cosmos, they are extremely common in Knitting, and almost all knitters will experience a black hole with almost every large project they knit. Despite this, black holes still cause knitters a great deal of discomfort. Following is the latest research on this scientific anomaly.

A typical sighting evolves in this way: A knitter working on a project may suddenly and inexplicably notice that despite knitting on the project for a long time, it shows no progress. Let's say it's a shawl I was knitting yesterday. I measured the shawl early in the day, then I knit a little bit in the morning while I drank my coffee, nailed a few rows on the bus on my way to work, and had a nice big knit in the evening. I know for a fact that I knit at least twenty rows on this shawl yesterday. I've even got witnesses.

The row gauge on this shawl is twenty-eight rows to four inches. If I've knit twenty rows, I should have gained some distance — at least two and a half inches, maybe three. It only stands to reason that if I knit, the shawl will get bigger. It didn't. I knit twenty rows and the shawl was exactly the same size. Exactly. There was no discernible difference in length or width. I measured. This is a classic expression of a knitting black hole: knitting and knitting, and making no progress.

Ineffective Black Hole Strategies

- Stuffing the garment in question into a grocery bag and hiding it in the back of your closet.
- Starting another project so that the black hole becomes emotionally insecure and gives up to keep you from withdrawing more love.
- Knitting on your project sort of roughly so that it gets the idea that you mean business.
- Overly emotional pleading and begging, indulging in hard liquor, throwing things about, or generally being immature.

Knitters have known about this phenomenon for a long time. The black hole of knitting is not new, and far better knitters than I have suffered deeply in its grip. So far, although many of us have tried many strategies, the only way to escape this phenomenon is time. If you put in time — not knitting time (that's completely irrelevant); I'm talking about waiting time — when your time is up, you are released from the black hole. I personally measured sleeves at twelve inches, knit 3,674 rows, still measured twelve inches, had a little lie-down and maybe a bit of a drunk-up and a temper tantrum, and suddenly I'm at more than fifteen inches without knitting another stitch. It's about doing your time and understanding that the knitting goddesses are choosing to play with as if you are a ratty little cat toy.

Some research by knitters has revealed that real black holes (the ones in the sky instead of in your knitting bag) are related to gravity. (*Disclaimer:* I'm a knitter, not an astrophysicist. You should not write a paper in science class based on the black hole theory I'm about to offer. In addition, if you're a student who does fail science because I'm wrong about this, you should know that there is no way that you'll be able to convince me that I'm responsible. Study your textbook.) So black holes are a gravity thing. Every object has a gravitational field. The more mass an object has (please remember, class, that mass is different from size), the harder it pulls on other things. Black holes (regardless of their size) have so much mass in one spot that they have an enormous gravitational pull — so big, in fact, that even light is pulled into them. (Hence the "blackness" of the hole.) That's a lot of gravity.

Now, sometimes knitting functions this way. (I choose to believe that some knits develop a wicked pull because they are so beautiful that they have a lot of knitterly gravity in one place, but science has yet to back me up on this.) In a knitting black hole, the yarn goes in but no length comes out, because the pull of the knitting is too great to allow it. (In the interest of complete honesty, science hasn't agreed on this, either.)

If you are experiencing the power of a knitting black hole, you have a problem, but I think I have a solution, beyond waiting for the hole to be done with you. It's another scientific theory, called *escape velocity*. If you're juggling and you throw a ball into the air, it'll go up for a little while because the force you've used to send it upward is greater than the force of gravity. The ball goes up, up, up until eventually the force sending it up becomes less than the force of gravity, and the ball is pulled back down. If, however, you had some sort of freaky superpower and you could hurl that ball upward — really heave it — then you might throw it so hard that it could escape the pull of the earth, enter space, and go on forever. This amount of force, the speed that it would take to beat the force of gravity, is called *escape velocity*.

Here on Earth, objects have more mass than on the moon, so things need to move faster here to escape the earth's gravitational pull than they would on the moon. A higher escape velocity is required here. Jupiter is so big that you'd need a super-fast velocity there, and black holes (both celestial and knitterly) have so much mass and, therefore, gravitational pull (or knitting mojo) that the escape velocity required to pull yourself or anything else out of the field of gravity is so huge that you . . . Well, you can only imagine that most encounters with a black hole end badly.

In order to escape a knitting black hole, you need a remarkable escape velocity. Escape = speed, and to really get out of the pull of the black hole, you have to knit as fast as you can. Then you might see some progress.

If it turns out that I'm correct about black holes in knitting, gravitational pull, and the way the universe is put together, I expect that knitters will finally have an alternative to having their poor chains yanked by an insubordinate, obdurate piece of mass-sucking knitting. We will be free at last. Just knit fast.

Groundbreaking work, really.

"Our happiest moments as tourists always seem to come when we stumble upon one thing while in pursuit of something else."

— **Lawrence Block**

PROCEED WITH CAUTION

CAUTION: Important Instruction
Studies have indicated that knitters are showing an alarming tendency to laugh at the knitting instruction "Join, being careful not to twist." One knitter was even overheard at Knit Night last week saying "I hate that instruction. It's so stupid. Everybody knows you have to check and see if the cast-on is twisted. It's like the sticker on a new hair dryer that says 'Do not immerse in water.' Totally lame."

Researchers then observed the mouthy knitter casting on two hundred stitches on a circular needle, joining it in a round, knitting three full rounds, and then fnding a twist in the original cast-on. The knitter declined to comment further as she got a rather large beer from the bar.

Studies conclude that double-checking a circular cast-on for a twist is not "totally lame" and that careful attention to this instruction can indeed prevent heartache and public displays of drunkenness.

NATURAL DISASTERS IN KNITTING

ONCE UPON A TIME, A NICE KNITTER — let's call her Knitter A — sat in her house, peacefully knitting a sweater. Knitter A thought she was shaping the shoulder. She knew she had done the decrease math correctly, she felt confident that she had corrected all of her errors as she went along, and she knew as surely as she knew her own name that she had gotten gauge down to the tiniest fraction of a stitch. (She had done four swatches.) Everything was perfect as she was finishing the top of the sweater; everything had come together and the knitting was sweet. Little did Knitter A know, however, that all of this meant nothing, that far away the knitting fates cackled as they watched from their place in destiny.

The fates knew something she did not: In another house there was another knitter — let's call her Knitter B — working on another sweater. Knitter B had been cavalier. Knitter B had not knitted a gauge swatch. Knitter B hadn't even read the instructions through before starting. She had substituted yarns and changed the stitch pattern, and one time, while she was doing her shoulder shaping and there had been two stitches left over in a bad spot, instead of figuring out what had gone wrong, as our diligent Knitter A would, Knitter B just knit two together twice.

What the fates knew, what made them giggle themselves just plain silly as they watched these knitters, was that Knitting has weather and seasons and no end of the knitting equivalent of tornadoes and earthquakes, which can pop up out of nowhere and wipe out a project. One such knitting disaster was coming now, and the fates rubbed their hands and watched, knowing that the two knitters had no idea what was going to happen next.

A wind had begun to blow in Knitting, and it was picking up speed. First it blew over Knitter B's house, acquiring knitting mojo as it traveled, and as it came over the knitter's basket, it blew warm, lovely knitting goodness all over it. Despite all odds, although Knitter B had tempted the fates and was completely undeserving and without a swatch, her sweater was now going to be wonderful. Certainly, the sweater would be doomed had this wind not begun to blow. But now? Now it was going to fit her perfectly. The stitch she had substituted was going to complement the yarn she had substituted more perfectly than peanut butter does jelly. True, the gauge she had ended up knitting was a little loose, but if she had done a swatch to gauge, the sweater would have gapped in the front. The sweater was going to make her look tall and take ten pounds off her figure every time she put it on and total strangers on the street were going to ask her where she got it. Just because this wind had blown, her project was going to be a knitting triumph of wool and wits.

As for Knitter A, she was screwed. The wind picked up speed as it moved across the land of Knitting and became a dangerous force. It careened across the Plains of Stockinette. It smashed through the Cable Mountains. It roared down the Hills of Garter. When it got to Knitter A's house, it was a full-on natural disaster. The wind blasted into the house and whipped across the knitting basket — and worst of all, even though Knitter A was sitting right there, sewing up the seams of her meticulously crafted sweater, she had no idea. The wind was silent and imperceptible. Knitter A felt nothing. As a matter of fact, she would never have even known that there had been a terrible wind in Knitting or that it had hit her house but for one circumstance.

Her beautiful pullover would not fit over her head.

Natural disasters in Knitting are common, violent, dangerous, and unpredictable. There are no warning systems, no horns, no radar, and no satellite spotting to aid in the face of them. We are defenseless.

We can be comforted only by knowing that disaster is out there and that sometimes it's nobody's fault when bad knits happen to good people or, more infuriatingly, when good knits happen to bad ones.

NO
4TH
TERM

WIN
WITH
WOOL

Save T
Wool

VOTE
FIBER

NATURAL

BLOCKING FLATS

KNITTERS
WITHOU

POLITICS

THE LAND OF KNITTING is a peaceful place. It has been suggested that this is because you need to put down your knitting needles in order to have a really good dust-up and also because nobody wants to see innocent yarn caught in the middle.

Nonetheless, although knitters are seldom reduced to violence, there are political matters that incite heated debate. These issues are perennial, and like matters of politics in the world beyond Knitting, they are best not brought up at dinner parties.

Acrylic versus Natural Fibers

Opponents in this fight can work up a really good head of steam. Primary arguments consist of hand-wash versus machine-wash (with the natural fiber camp pulling out machine-washable/dryable superwash wool when things start getting loud). The acrylic camp then counters with the cost of natural fibers, at which point the natural fiber types start suggesting that clothing that melts in a fire might not be a good idea. Someone on the acrylic side replies that wool itches, and then at some point someone calls someone else a fiber snob. This argument resolves rapidly if a clear-thinking individual responds with a big tray of brownies.

SAFETY TIP

Many knitters knit baby items out of synthetic yarns because they are inexpensive and very washable. (These are fine traits in a baby yarn.) Synthetic fibers are highly flammable, however, and can cause severe burns if they catch fire and melt. Wool, on the other hand, is naturally flame retardant. Synthetic fibers should not be used for items that accompany babies and children at night (such as crib blankets); they should be reserved for times when children are supervised.

The Choice Debate: Circular Needles versus Straight Needles

This argument usually resolves with both sides agreeing that they respect a knitter's right to choose. There are too many strong feelings in both camps and too many excellent points (both literally and figuratively) to be made for both cases. The needle debate provides a good time to consider how really clever it is to argue when people are holding pointy sticks.

Sock Issues

"Toe up" versus "cuff down," two circular needles versus double-pointed needles, and how long the ribbing should be to hold up a dress sock are arguments really best not brought up in public. If you can't avoid the debate, frequently use the phrase "not that there's anything wrong with that." Trust me.

Enemies of the State

As difficult as it may be for knitters to fully comprehend, there are people on the earth not only who are knit-neutral or who do not knit, but who actively dislike knitting. (Sit down for a few minutes and put your head between your knees if you feel at all dizzy after reading that.) These people go beyond the bewildered muggles who surround us every day; they are truly knit-hostile.

These are the people who tell you — and mean it — to get rid of your stash. These are the people who ask you not to knit because when you knit, they feel they don't have enough of your attention (despite the fact that you look them dead in the eye while they're talking). These are the people, my friends, who will tell you that they would rather you not knit because they find it irritating or distracting to be around your flashing needles. These people might tell you that they think it's ridiculous to knit socks when you can get them for a dollar, and these people think all wool itches. (Actually, there are Jacuzzis that are more itchy than some high-grade merinos.) These people are the enemy, and there is nothing you can do to fight them except to avoid marrying them and to remove them from the Christmas sweater list. They are never going to understand you.

December 30
Dear Mum,
Guess freaking what? Aunt Sue didn't like the hat I made her. Andy and I trucked down to her place on Boxing Day with the hat all wrapped up in tissue paper and the good wrapping paper, and she opened it up and didn't like it. I could tell. She gave it a sniffy little look and said it was "nice," and then she opened a box from Sarah and went nuts over some totally lame store-bought scarf. STORE-BOUGHT!
I know she never likes anything I make, but I'm really disappointed — disappointed and furious, actually. Andy thinks I'm a fool for spending any effort on her gift at all, especially after he found that sweater he gave her last year lining that yappy little dog's bed, and I've got to admit that I see his point. Every year I try to get her something she likes and it never works. This year, though, I really thought that if I knit her a hat, she would be pleased. It's soft, it's beautiful, it's handmade, and it's the exact stinking color of her coat. What's not to like?
I fumed about it all the way home, trying to figure

out why I was so mad. It didn't bother me at all two years ago when she said the antique mirror I gave her was "an interesting choice," and unlike Andy, I don't care how many of our gifts she gives to the dog. Why was it burning me up this time?

It wasn't until I was sitting and knitting tonight that I totally got it. I'm mad because I didn't just give her a hat. I gave her the gift of my time, a chunk of my life. I gave great whacks of time to try to please that harpy — hundreds and hundreds of minutes concentrated on that hat, a span of my days on this earth holding wool and needles on her behalf. Time, Mum, I gave her time — time that I could have spent doing just about anything else other than covering her weasel head.

Next year, it's a store-bought fruitcake for Aunt Sue.

Alice

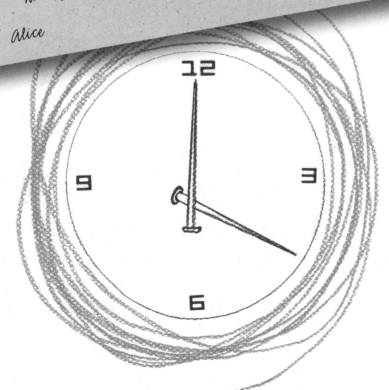

For the Committed Non-Knitter:
What Knitters Like

Occasionally a non-knitter has to give a knitter a present. I offer the following card to help eliminate the disappointment and frustration in both the giver and the giftee alike. Copy it and distribute it at will to non-knitters, especially at the holidays.

Dear _____

If you have received this card, it is because you know and likely love a knitter who feels that you could use some help. Note: Defensiveness will help no one. We're not blaming you for last year's gifts. After all, lots of people really like those nifty hand blenders. You were under a lot of strain, what with knowing that your knitter was probably going to give you something unique, such as hand-knit dress socks. The important thing is that we move forward together now. Buying gifts for knitters may seem complex, but if you come to understand a few things about your knitter, you will do better.

1. Your knitter has a lot of yarn because she likes it. This means that MORE YARN is always a good gift. (We know it appears that she has more than enough. You may also have heard your knitter say that she has too much yarn. She is lying. Sometimes a knitter says such things to a non-knitter to make the non-knitter feel she is sympathetic to the idea that there is too much yarn, but knitters don't believe it.

2. Knitters like to make things out of yarn themselves. This is why the sweater you are thinking about buying is not going to go over as well as you hope. Even though it is made of yarn, and even though your knitter may make lots of sweaters, those from the store come with your knitter's favorite part already done.

3. Next to yarn, the best present you can give a knitter is time to knit. Take her kids to the park, rent a movie (no subtitles please; it's too hard to read a chart and subtitles), or make dinner for your knitter. She will be thrilled. (Naturally, this reaction is only enhanced if you give your knitter both yarn and time.)

Thank you for your consideration. Please look for other helpful cards in this series, such as "Hand-Knits and How to Wash Them Yourself" and "Why Cleaning the Bathroom Makes You Really Sexy."

JUSTICE SYSTEM: WHEN BAD KNITS HAPPEN TO GOOD KNITTERS

LIKE EVERYWHERE ELSE, Knitting has criminals. They are usually sweaters, but the occasional pair of socks gets out of hand as well. Knitters do, however, have a system of justice. We look out for each other, and if someone is taking a criminal amount of heat from a project, justice is served. Think of it as a neighborhood watch.

Hear ye, hear ye! Due process was served yesterday in a local yarn shop, wherein the knitter (whose name is withheld under the Yarn Offender's Act) did show her intarsia jacket to her fellow knitters and gave testimony on the events that had transpired in the case to date.

The jacket in question was accused of "ugliness, strange holes in funny places, and being remarkably ill fitting." The knitter stated that she had put a great deal of effort into the knitting of the intarsia garment, although even on cross-examination she could not answer the question "What were you thinking?" The jury advocated that the jacket be prosecuted to the fullest possible extent of Knitting law, considering that it seemed to have an almost mystic pull on the knitter, that the length of its arms violated the human form, that it had an odd swelling in the arse area, and that the knitter was still planning on wearing it in public. The knitter also admitted under duress that she had woven in many ends on the jacket and had even continued to block it in good faith, despite the many months of gauge abuse she had suffered at its hands. The witnesses were unmoved by her claims that she was not at fault for the dizzingly horrific color combinations that she said resulted from an altered mental state caused by a yarn sale.

Following a brief discussion of whether the yarn could be rehabilitated, the knitter's jacket was convicted of all charges and sentenced to death by garbage can. A stay of execution was suggested by a number of jurors, who attempted to convert the jacket to a pillow, and one member offered clemency and a new home to the accused, but the trash was taken to the curb before the jacket had the opportunity to corrupt another knitter.

Answering the cries of "There's no such thing as bad knitting!" from the moved members of the gallery, the judge wrote in her court statement: "Unfortunately, it was a miserable piece of ugly knitting and this court took immense pleasure in heaving it into the garbage can and watching as it was subsequently covered with coffee grounds. In a just society, citizens must be protected from the dangers of hurtful projects that have no hope of ever regretting their behavior."

The knitter in question cried softly as the sentence was carried out, but was seen shortly after with some new yarn. The jury supported her, saying, "We're all just so happy that she can finally have some closure and move on. No knitter needs to be treated that way."

From: andyoko@sympatico.cast

Subject: Alice has a new hobby

Date: March 2 10:49:04 PM EDT

To: stacey@yahoo.knit, crazygy@erg.castst, blackroses@hotmail.knit, ronnie567@hotmail.knit, shorty_shorty@yahoo.knit, bobsdad@yahoo.knit, kruppert@cox.castst, pete5678@index.cast, rexxsmith@yahoo.knit, rsbeaceh@gmail.knit, bcat@hotmail.knit, joedump@thebigone.knit, rachellrg@hotmail.knit

Hi everyone. Guess who? I know it's been a really long time since I talked with any of you. I guess it's been awhile since university. How's it going?

I wanted to e-mail and ask if anyone needs some knitted slippers. My wife's learned to knit and she's on a bit of a jag.

Let me know. We have lots (seriously)!

Andy

CAUTION: *Knitting Jag*

PROCEED WITH CAUTION

Every once in a while a knitter comes down with a spectacular case of knitting jag, which is just like a toddler's food jag. In a food jag, a three-year-old eats nothing but yellow beans and scrambled eggs for weeks on end with no ill effect while his mother comes unhinged about the possibility of the child contracting scurvy caused by a diet that consists of only two yellow foods.

With knitting, usually a garment has one go in it. By the time you've finished it, you've really got no more of the item in you. (Of course, this is the entire basis for the difficulty with knitting a second sock or mitten.) With a knitting jag, however, a knitter finds a pattern she thinks is charming and knits it up and in so doing discovers more of its charms. In fact,

each knitting of the item is as enchanting as the last.

As a general rule, knitting jags occur with items that pay off quickly: slippers, mittens, scarves, hats. (This is not always

the case, however. I would rather not discuss the "festival shawl" episode of 2003. It was a dark and strange time.) The knitter comes to memorize (or at least accept) the pattern, starts getting pretty happy about how fast the objects are piling up . . . and somehow, it just doesn't get old for him. It's as though the knitter must exhaust all of the cleverness in the pattern before he can move on.

The only downside to knitting jags is that they never end in a tidy way.

Usually, just when a knitter has accepted that she is exclusively a ribbed-mitten knitter, has come to understand that she will never show any interest in anything else for the rest of her days, and has bought enough yarn to make 302 pairs of mittens of various sizes and colors in the cherished rib pattern . . . she tires of mittens. It's another of knitting's little jokes.

"Stop worrying about the potholes in the road and celebrate the journey."

— **Fitzhugh Mullan**

Three Things
That Knitters Would Like the Other Residents of the World to Understand

1 We can knit and listen at the same time. Just because I'm knitting doesn't mean that you don't have my attention. I'm multitasking.

2 The best gift you can buy me is yarn. Do not think that because I have a lot of yarn, I don't need more. I have a lot of yarn because I like it.

3 Even though I'm cursing and gritting my teeth so hard that you could crack diamonds between them, I assure you that I like knitting. I think it's fun, and I am relaxing.

Useful Translation

13, 14, 15, 16 . . .

I'm counting. I'm in the middle of a row and I'm following a chart. If you continue to speak to me — even though I have answered your question ("Did you know the dryer is on fire?") with a string of numbers, which clearly indicates that I cannot be disturbed at present — I shall have no choice but to hold you entirely responsible when I have to count these stitches 345 more times. It won't be pretty.

Deadline Knitting
and How to Get It All Done

- **No social knitting.** Talking and enjoying human company only slow you down.

- **Sequester yourself.** Limiting contact with the outside world can also be of use. Unplugging the phone and disconnecting your Internet can help reduce distractions. Naturally, if you have any children, they will need to go.

- **Discontinue other activities.** I suggest letting go of housework and laundry first.

- **Inform people.** Tell your friends and family that you are going to attempt the impossible. Tell them it will go better for them if they are on your side. Tell them that the more they cooperate, the sooner it will be over and you will be able to resume your normal family role. (If they doubt you, release all of the tears you have been holding back. Show them your pain.)

HEALTH WARNINGS: COMMON AILMENTS IN THE LAND OF KNITTING

STARTITIS IS A COMMON ILLNESS in Knitting and one for which there has never been a treatment or vaccine. Most knitters will have several bouts of the ailment during their residence in Knitting, and it occurs as frequently among new knitters as traveler's trot occurs among visitors to other parts of the world. (Fortunately, it's a lot more glamorous than its non-knitting equivalent.)

Starting a new project is thrilling. In that moment you hold in your hands not merely yarn, needles, and the pattern; you hold the world of possibility. This new project can be the perfect one, the project with no mistakes! This is the one that will fit perfectly, this is the one that will come together like magic.

This feeling is addictive. Personal causes of startitis vary, but for me, it is always a reflection of worry in another area. I always get startitis as deadlines in the rest of my life approach. When the time draws near for me to crack the whip and meet a work or family deadline, I can often be found on the couch with yarn and needles, starting project after project after project, all of them eventually (or immediately) falling short of satisfaction, which drives me to another. For me, a case of startitis balances the need to finish up something else. If you are currently in the grip of startitis, look for emotional needs that you might be meeting by casting on new projects, then congratulate yourself for managing to come up with such an interesting way to balance your life.

SYMPTOMS: The first indication that a knitter has contracted startitis is a general and vague discomfort or ennui with knitting already on the needles. Whether the knitter has two or twelve projects on the go, she begins to feel a certain creeping malaise. Projects that were flying now inch along, and the knitter may be heard to exclaim that she finds all her work "boring." She is not, however, bored with knitting overall (such as with whiplash; see page 134) and shows a keen interest in any knitting that is not on her needles at that moment. As the knitter grows increasingly uncomfortable, she may be found repeatedly stash diving for "something good." Left unattended, the knitter may sit very happily in a pile of new projects, each just cast on.

TREATMENT: Many knitters have found some relief by limiting the number of needles they own. Some deliberately hamper themselves by carrying only one project when they are out of the house. (*Caution:* Knitters in the grip of startitis have been known to nip into a yarn shop on their lunch hour in order to purchase more yarn and needles to "scratch the itch." It may be necessary to leave credit cards and cash at home.) Assuming that the knitter is not made unhappy (or unable to pay the rent), startitis can be allowed to run its course; most knitters will self-correct eventually.

PROGNOSIS: Excellent, though there may be some permanent damage to the empty needle supply in the knitter's house. (One of the most surprising side effects of repeated cases of startitis is owning thirty-two pairs of number 7 needles because new needles must be purchased during every case.)

Finish-It-Upitis

This is an extraordinarily rare disease of knitting and one that many knitters wish they would contract. Unlike the normal impulse to finish a few things and free up the needles (this urge seldom lasts long), finish-it-upitis truly grips a knitter.

SYMPTOMS: The primary symptom is the seemingly relentless need to finish projects under way. A knitter will show little or no interest in new yarn, new projects, or new plans, even when sale yarn is waved under her nose. In severe cases of finish-it-upitis, a knitter may even turn her back on beloved yarns priced at 50 percent off. Very rarely this disease is complicated by an urge to "stash cull," but evidence of this remains anecdotal.

TREATMENT: None. In fact, only yarn shop owners are at all interested in finding a cure. The rest of us are trying to catch it.

PROGNOSIS: Excellent. Most knitters recover very quickly — in fact, so quickly that often nothing at all is finished. (Good time is made for a while, though, and who doesn't want that?)

Whiplash

Whiplash is an infirmity afflicting a knitter who has recently completed an enormous wonder of work, often under deadline. When a huge shawl or intricate sweater or even a pair of socks knit at a speed that consumed the knitter's waking hours for some time is finished, the knitter suddenly finds little strength for knitting.

SYMPTOMS: These include a seeming loss of appetite for yarn and knitting. The knitter may stand in front of the stash or yarn shop shelves for hours but find nothing appealing. This is usually accompanied by some measure of distress for the knitter, who, despite not wanting to knit, can imagine no other way of living.

TREATMENT: Treatment for whiplash is twofold. First, the knitter needs reassurance that the will to knit will return and that despite not knitting right this minute, she is still a knitter. Application of wool compresses can help; yarn fumes can speed recovery, as can exposing the knitter to simple, straightforward projects with none of the deadlines or intricacy of the project that put her over the edge. Some researchers report encouraging results from using therapeutic garter-stitch washcloths or simple scarves.

PROGNOSIS: Excellent. Most knitters recover completely from whiplash, usually about halfway through knitting a garter-stitch scarf. Recovery is likely complete when the knitter pronounces the garter-stitch project "boring" or makes plans to attend a yarn sale. *Warning:* Knitters recovering from whiplash often suffer a yarn seizure if they return to the yarn shop too quickly after their illness or with too much money. Care should be taken to protect their budget from the damage that can be done when the will to knit (and stash) returns, often with a vengeance.

Second Sock Syndrome

Second Sock Syndrome (SSS) is an extremely common affliction in Knitting and most knitters will contract one or more forms of the disease at some point in their knitting lives. In fact, so common is this syndrome that by the time most knitters have completed a few socks (which may or may not match), they have accepted that they will live with a mild, chronic form of the condition all of their knitting days. Every knitter who contracts SSS will be afflicted with a slightly different form of the illness.

Although almost all sock knitters acquire SSS at some point, it is not always an illness that troubles them while they have it, which may have something to do with the lack of any real research into a cure. Product knitters may be deeply troubled by even the occasional flare-up, which can result in the failure to come up with a timely pair of socks, while process knitters with the disease often live completely normal lives, even while leaving scads of lonely single socks in their wake. Whether or not a case of SSS keeps you up at night is a good indication of your knitting personality type (see page 8).

Viral SSS

Much like the common cold, viral SSS (VSSS) occurs frequently among knitters, and most knitters will contract it several times during their knitting lifetime. The mildest form of Second Sock Syndrome, VSSS is mostly just uncomfortable. Having VSSS once may confer some immunity, as indicated by the fact that most knitters eventually do go on to knit second socks, and even isolated cases resulting in a single sock do not indicate similar failure in future sock-knitting attempts.

SYMPTOMS: These include finding the second sock considerably less charming than the first, and perhaps referring to it using adjectives such as *fiddly* and *annoying*. (This assumes that the knitter in question described the first sock with terms such as *charming* and *intriguing*. Dislike of the first sock may be the first indication of malignant SSS. See page 138.) The knitter may consider beginning other projects, but will likely return to the single sock out of a sense of duty and a desire to have a pair.

TREATMENT: Symptomatic. Occasionally, starting another project helps, although it is generally not recommended. Other knitters may support recovery by refusing to go along with the knitter's wish that everyone overlook the first sock of the pair.

PROGNOSIS: Excellent. Although some knitters take many months to recover and knit the second sock, almost all knitters eventually do go on to produce a pair of socks.

Bacterial SSS

Bacterial SSS (BSSS) is more serious. We suspect that it may be spread by bacteria living on the wool of the socks themselves. It has resulted in many single socks left scattered across the world. Because sock knitters in all climates are affected, the bacterium responsible seems impervious to heat and cold.

SYMPTOMS: These include the knitter's use of advanced adjectives such as *stupid* and *dumbass* in reference to the first sock. The knitter may repeatedly find herself in front of the stash, looking for any project to begin, as if helplessly and inexplicably drawn there. (*Note:* This is an important point for differential diagnosis. Viral SSS victims remain fixated on sock projects, while bacterial SSS sufferers look for any project at all to replace the second sock.)

TREATMENT: Antibacterial therapies may be needed. Reducing exposure to the bacteria by reducing contact with additional sock yarn has had some effect. The most efficient treatment is for the patient to carry in her knitting bag only the single sock and the yarn for its mate. When the knitter needs to knit, only the sock is available and the second sock may be accomplished. (Knitters receiving limitation therapy may become desperate during their treatment. Local yarn shops should be advised of the likelihood of a knitter attempting to purchase forty-seven skeins of sock yarn and four pairs of double-pointed needles to "take the edge off.") Wherever possible, access to yarn should be limited until bacterial levels are under control and the second sock is complete. Due to the sneaky nature of knitters under duress, this treatment has found only limited success.

PROGNOSIS: Fair. The sock knitter may recover and a pair of socks is still a possible goal, though recovery may be so slow as to result in several single socks strewn about the stash zone before a pair appears.

Malignant SSS

This variant of the disease is terminal. The second sock will not survive and, in fact, may never be cast on. There is no treatment for malignant SSS (MSSS), and it leaves a vicious swath of single socks in its path. In this most virulent form of SSS, the sock knitter is forced to endure a painful outcome: She cannot cast on the second sock, yet she cannot admit this and is forced to keep the unfinished project in her possession for many, many years.

SYMPTOMS: The knitter no longer uses adjectives or any other words to refer to the second sock and may instead appear dazed and say "What sock?" even as she is immediately surrounded by immense piles of single socks.

TREATMENT: None. The knitter should be supported in her delusions to prevent malignant SSS from spreading to other areas of her knitting.

PROGNOSIS: Poor. Short of getting a cold one-legged pirate's address, there is no happy ending. Damage may be minimized by keeping the knitter from starting up with mitten knitting.

Yarnesia

This is the inability of a knitter to recall yarn or projects that have been stashed in her home. Its onset may be due to genuine forgetfulness (many stashes are cultivated over decades, and who could really remember all that?) or occasionally can be attributed to trauma. I have discovered countless sweaters and blankets and one particularly painful single glove crammed into the back of the linen closet, dusty and consigned to a dark fate. Each item had something horribly wrong with it . . . and I didn't remember a single one until they tumbled out during excavation.

PESTS

THERE ARE A FEW SPECIES of knitters who remain pests, but the hunting of these animals is frowned upon by the generally gentle society of Knitting.

The Long-Tailed Stash Scooper

This breed of knitter walks the line between a pest and a danger and can be a wily predator. Driven to spoil the fun of other fiberists, the long-tailed stash scooper appears with stunning regularity at yarn shops and fiber festivals and quickly purchases the very things that you want. No one knows how the scooper is able to do this, but rest assured that if you are going to buy that blue wool for a sweater and you put it down for a minute to find your wallet, with shocking speed, the stash scooper will appear out of nowhere, scoop up the yarn, and have it at the cash register before you can say "Holy highland sheep!"

Stash scoopers also prey on the undecided and will often make a yarn decision for you if you walk away from the yarn for a moment to think about it. Not at all rare and very quick and dangerous, the long-tailed stash scooper appears in all fiber environments and continues to threaten the stash shopping of knitters everywhere. Current defenses include clutching your selections to your chest while shopping and making snap decisions.

The Free-Range Enabler

Caution should be used around this dangerous breed of knitter, for the damage such an enabler inflicts on the pocketbooks of knitters caught in her web can be devastating. These knitters may be low-stashers themselves or simply stashers thwarted by a lack of space or money, but whatever the motivation, their *modus operandi* remains the same: The enabler spots a knitter in the wild and advances. (Because an enabler is often known to the knitter, usually the victim is not alarmed and does not even run.) Once within striking distance, the enabler begins to sing the praises of some knitting product within procuring range of the knitter. Within moments, the innocent knitter has been helped into purchasing something that she normally would have been able to resist. The goal of an enabler is to get the hapless victim to spend a great deal of money, therefore creating a vicarious experience for the enabler, who walks away having had the joy of a yarn purchase without the resulting damage to her budget. In short, she gets all of the fun with none of the responsibility.

The enabler attack can be discerned from the approach of another knitting buddy (friendly fire) in the following ways.

- The enabler will frequently ask you to hold, stroke, or examine a product that she herself is not purchasing. (A knitter who tries to get you to buy some of what she is buying is just sharing good fortune.)
- Among a dozen knitters who go together to a yarn sale, the enabler is the one who, when the dust settles and the car trunk is stuffed, has the most satisfied expression and the smallest number of purchases.
- An enabler almost always has exquisite taste and an exceptional gift for finding your perfect yarn/fiber/fleece/book/spinning wheel. In fact, many enablers have what my mother calls "champagne taste and a beer pocket." This makes complete sense. It would be much harder to get you to buy crap you don't like. (This points out a big difference between an enabler and friendly fire. A knitting buddy often just wants you to buy what she likes. An enabler intuitively knows your heart's yarn longing.)

- **Fifty percent or more of an enabler's conversation** starters are "Have you seen this?" or "Touch this!" or the deadly "Look what I found!"

- **Enablers are bold.** They don't gently "suggest" anything. They tell you to buy things. They say, "Get it." They put it in your basket and declare it's a steal. They're aggressive, they're relentless, and they've found me some of the best yarn I've ever purchased. It's a love/hate relationship.

The Skanky Knitted Bikini

There have been many attempts to control the number of skanky knitted bikinis over the years, but sporadic patterns continue to crop up and alarm knitters from time to time. Control measures have included pointing out that the stupid things don't stay up when they get wet, which thus reduces the usefulness of the bikini as a bathing costume; advising knitters that the tan received when wearing a skanky bikini can be really freaking weird, depending on the gauge of the knitter and how big the holes are; and siccing mothers from all over on the wearers of these bikinis to point out that they are . . . well . . . skanky.

Volunteer programs have been somewhat successful in introducing less skanky knitted swimwear to the environment, but overall, the skanky bikini remains a pest.

Hockey Sweaters

It is my opinion that everything possible should be done to reduce the incidence of the hand-knit hockey sweater. Sightings are rare, but not rare enough. Though I am a Canadian and thus believe that the sport of hockey is fine and noble, and while in theory, adding knitwear to hockey makes it only more noble, I must point out, for the sake of anyone quite taken with the frosty but romantic idea of clothing your handsome hockey player with a hand-knit jersey, that the sweater will be worn during actual hockey play. If the idea of any piece of your knitting being used for an actual game does not offend you to the core of your being, then all we can do to help you understand is send you to your local rink to smell a genuine hockey equipment bag.

ENDANGERED SPECIES

FEW CREATURES IN KNITTING ever become truly extinct, though many teeter on the edge before being rediscovered and yanked back from the brink.

The Low Stasher

True low stashers are exceptionally rare. There are many knitters who appear to be low stashers, but they have petite stashes only because of artificial restrictions. Perhaps they live in a small house or have a small income, perhaps the stash they do have is misunderstood by those who live with them and they've found that being temporarily low-stashing helps keep the peace (and the closet space). Whatever the reason for their restraint, those who would have more if they could are not true low stashers.

When bred true, the low stasher is a knitter who genuinely feels no need to stockpile wool in vast quantities. She does not fear a wool blight, she does not find yarn inspiring to have around in groups, she prefers her stash sparse. Many low stashers speak of being overwhelmed by vast amounts of yarn in their homes and find having a small or nonexistent stash spiritually lightening. Should you encounter a true low stasher, admire her greatly. You may never meet another one.

The Wild Argyle

There once was a brave and noble time when scores of argyle-sock knitters roamed the world of knitting freely with many colors of yarn. Even people who have done no other sort of knitting recall free-range occurrences in the days of argyle, though the once common diamonds are seldom seen on the needles of modern knitters. Several factors have influenced the shrinking numbers of the wild argyle. Argyles are worked flat, and the land for knitters who will sew seams is ever diminishing in these days of the circular needle. In addition, the wild argyle dines solely on the rare intarsia flower, and few knitters cultivate it in their gardens because it has an undeserved reputation for being difficult to manage.

The Long Scottish Kilt Hose

This knee-length men's sock, often elaborately cabled, especially during mating season, has had a hard go in recent decades. Although I have spotted some in the wild and even knit a pair at one time, the extreme shortage of the urban bagpiper continues to be a problem for the once thriving kilt hose.

Super Soakers

Soakers are knitted woolen diaper covers used specifically for covering cloth diapers. Even though these covers are easy to make, easy to use, and far kinder to the planet than two years of plastic and paper diapers per child, the super soaker has fallen out of vogue. This could be due to its need for at least occasional washing.

Elizabeth Zimmermann

Funny, intelligent, and helpful, Elizabeth Zimmermann (August 10, 1910–November 30, 1999) is remembered for giving knitting back to knitters, infusing it with intelligence and an uncommon amount of common sense. This citizen of Knitting freed countless poor souls from the grip of patterns that they didn't like and couldn't understand, and her pithy, straightforward manner of describing knitting technique and ideas encouraged knitters actually to think about what they were doing.

When Elizabeth wasn't raising our knitting IQ, she was thinking herself, and her wonderfully intriguing patterns leave most knitters (and non-knitters) wondering what an incredible place it must have been inside her head. My favorite is the Baby Surprise Sweater, in which you work back and forth to create a piece of knitting resembling a manta ray more than a sweater, but when it's finished and you flip and fold it like origami, it stuns everyone nearby (and likely the knitter herself) by suddenly becoming a small and elegant sweater.

Elizabeth's books are patterns, help, thoughts, drawing, and writing about knitting and her remarkable life. When she died, the *New York Times* ran an obituary for her, a rare honor for a woman whose claim to fame was that she was good with wool. I never knew Elizabeth, but I still miss her.

January 17

Dear Mum,

I've been thinking about writing this letter for a while. I send you all of these bits and pieces of my life (and these days I send you hats and mittens and scarves too) and every time the topic of my knitting comes around, I feel you flinch a little. (I know the way I felt about that guy in the band when I was seventeen never really caught on with you either, but I think you pretended to be happy for me.) I've gone around and around with it and I think I know what's bothering you. I have become not just someone who knits, but a knitter, and maybe you feel that by becoming a knitter, I've somehow let feminism down — that partaking in a domestic art is a step backward, that when I sit and knit, I'm transporting humanity back to a time when women were ornamental and homebound and men were powerful and decisive. I think you worry that a woman can't possibly be taken seriously with yarn in her hands, and I know what you mean, because it's got to mean something that it's still mostly women who knit.

My first reflex is to say to you: Isn't this what feminism is about? Hasn't the whole effort been about making it so that women can choose their activities and not be forced by society into a gender role that creates a narrow idea of what a woman is? When I was in university I thought that feminism was about not allowing women to be limited: women at home, women in the workplace, women who are doctors and mothers and artists and welders. To me, feminism is about choice and opportunity and the right to choose how I'll spend my time and the necessity to prevent someone who sees my gender from making assumptions about what I'm capable of accomplishing. That fits with the whole knitting thing. I can do something traditionally feminine without being traditionally feminine. Feminism is about choice, right?

Then I thought some more and I realized that while my feminism is often about choice, your feminism is about

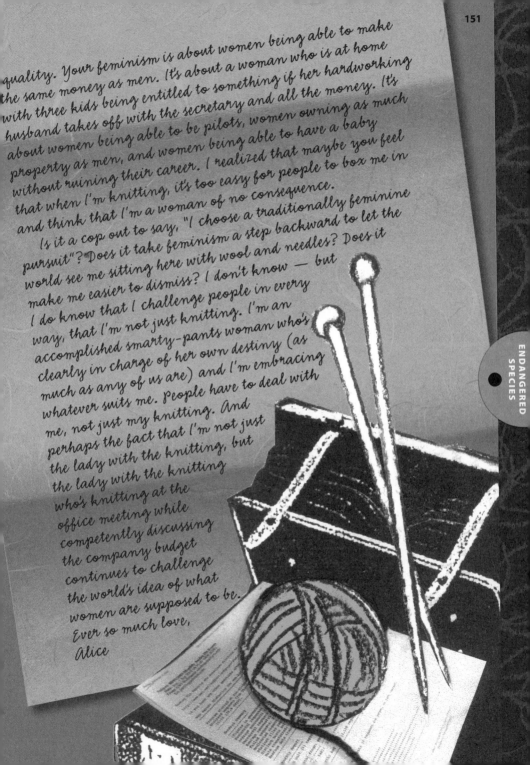

quality. Your feminism is about women being able to make the same money as men. It's about a woman who is at home with three kids being entitled to something if her hardworking husband takes off with the secretary and all the money. It's about women being able to be pilots, women owning as much property as men, and women being able to have a baby without ruining their career. I realized that maybe you feel that when I'm knitting, it's too easy for people to box me in and think that I'm a woman of no consequence.

Is it a cop out to say, "I choose a traditionally feminine pursuit"? Does it take feminism a step backward to let the world see me sitting here with wool and needles? Does it make me easier to dismiss? I don't know — but I do know that I challenge people in every way, that I'm not just knitting. I'm an accomplished smarty-pants woman who's clearly in charge of her own destiny (as much as any of us are) and I'm embracing whatever suits me. People have to deal with me, not just my knitting. And perhaps the fact that I'm not just the lady with the knitting, but the lady with the knitting who's knitting at the office meeting while competently discussing the company budget continues to challenge the world's idea of what women are supposed to be.

Ever so much love,

Alice

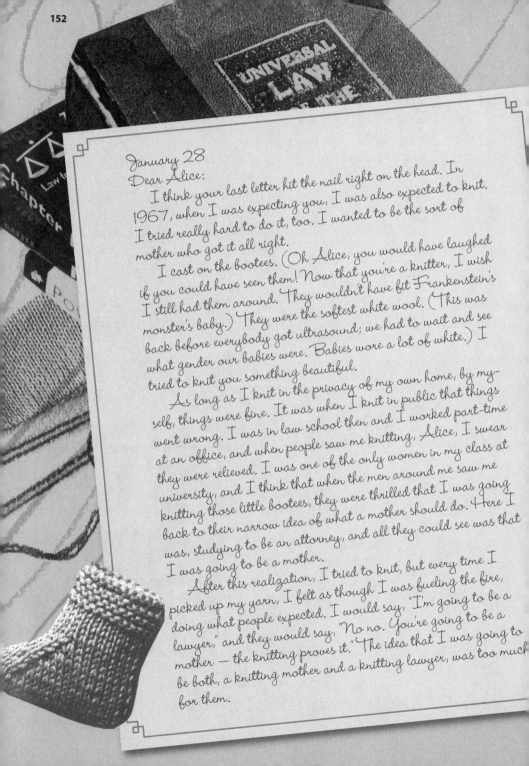

January 28

Dear Alice:

I think your last letter hit the nail right on the head. In 1967, when I was expecting you, I was also expected to knit. I tried really hard to do it, too. I wanted to be the sort of mother who got it all right.

I cast on the bootees. (Oh Alice, you would have laughed if you could have seen them! Now that you're a knitter, I wish I still had them around. They wouldn't have fit Frankenstein's monster's baby.) They were the softest white wool. (This was back before everybody got ultrasound; we had to wait and see what gender our babies were. Babies wore a lot of white.) I tried to knit you something beautiful.

As long as I knit in the privacy of my own home, by myself, things were fine. It was when I knit in public that things went wrong. I was in law school then and I worked part-time at an office, and when people saw me knitting, Alice, I swear they were relieved. I was one of the only women in my class at university, and I think that when the men around me saw me knitting those little bootees, they were thrilled that I was going back to their narrow idea of what a mother should do. Here I was, studying to be an attorney, and all they could see was that I was going to be a mother.

After this realization, I tried to knit, but every time I picked up my yarn, I felt as though I was fueling the fire, doing what people expected. I would say, "I'm going to be a lawyer," and they would say, "No no. You're going to be a mother — the knitting proves it." The idea that I was going to be both, a knitting mother and a knitting lawyer, was too much for them.

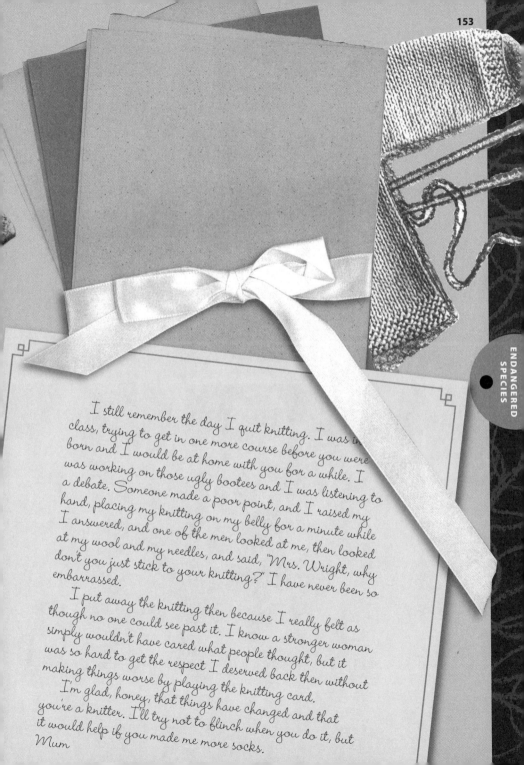

I still remember the day I quit knitting. I was in class, trying to get in one more course before you were born and I would be at home with you for a while. I was working on those ugly bootees and I was listening to a debate. Someone made a poor point, and I raised my hand, placing my knitting on my belly for a minute while I answered, and one of the men looked at me, then looked at my wool and my needles, and said, "Mrs. Wright, why don't you just stick to your knitting?" I have never been so embarrassed.

I put away the knitting then because I really felt as though no one could see past it. I know a stronger woman simply wouldn't have cared what people thought, but it was so hard to get the respect I deserved back then without making things worse by playing the knitting card.

I'm glad, honey, that things have changed and that you're a knitter. I'll try not to flinch when you do it, but it would help if you made me more socks.

Mum

SOCIAL CUSTOMS: ETIQUETTE IN THE LAND OF KNITTING

AS KNITTERS FREQUENTLY MINGLE with ordinary people and move in and out of knitting neighborhoods as they journey, these question often come up: Where is it okay to knit? Are there times when it's rude? Is it ever in poor taste? I've had knitters tell me that their spouses believe they are robbed of attention by knitting or that their bosses think they aren't listening when they knit or that they were asked not to knit in church. Clearly, we're looking for a few rules here, so I've given it some thought.

Where You Can Knit

- Anywhere, anytime in the land of Knitting. It's always permitted while you're within Knitting's borders: in yarn shops, guilds, or designated knitting areas. A place becomes a designated knitting area as soon as more than three knitters inhabit it.

- Anytime you are not interacting with other humans or the interaction is casual: at the movies (assuming you're using quiet needles and you aren't swearing at a cable), on public transit of any kind, waiting in line or for an appointment, at sporting events (assuming you're a spectator).

Where You Shouldn't Knit

Knitting is usually in poor taste when your full attention is required, when you're being paid for your full attention, when you're attending a ceremonial event, when the conditions are formal or somber, or when another person actually may be injured in a knitting-related accident. Don't knit:

- **At a funeral** (unless it's a knitter's funeral)
- **During an intense negotiation** in the boardroom
- **On the floor** of the stock exchange
- **During an argument** with your spouse, boss, or child
- **Anytime the space** you are in is too small or crowded for knitting, such as during rush hour on a bus, when it is conceivable that a lurch of the vehicle could impale your standing-mate on a fine metal sock needle

Even in places where knitting is in good taste, remember that the activity can be rude if it demands that you disengage from your guests or friends by consulting a chart or counting out loud. Such situations call for plain knitting.

All visitors and residents of Knitting at some point learn these rules. It's important to observe them and not to anger the knitting goddess or the yarn fates. Knitters are not always quite sure how these are offended, but we do know this: Their vengeance and fury are swift, and, should you attract either, mighty, cruel, and pointy.

Yesterday's Best and Worst...
Exchange-traded funds, latest
Thursday's best performers

KNITTING SPORTS

A SPORT IS DEFINED by my Oxford Concise Dictionary as "a physically and mentally challenging activity carried out with a recreational purpose for competition, self-enjoyment, to attain excellence, for the development of a skill, or some combination of these."

The more I read this definition, the more I can't believe that we've been arguing for years about whether knitting is an art or a craft. Clearly, according to this definition, knitting is a sport.

Describing knitting as a sport goes a long way toward making us less crazy or obsessed in the eyes of the rest of the world. People accept passion for a sport, and if you put knitting in this context, you no longer have to explain why you find it so interesting. Sports are interesting. If thousands of people can gather in stadiums all over the world and watch grown men in tight pants try to move a ball from one end of the grass to the other, then surely a person can develop an interest in watching a loop of yarn move from one needle to another. It's really all a matter of perspective. If knitting is a sport, then you don't have to explain why you have a needle collection, swift, or ball winder. Sports have equipment. You don't have to explain why you have so many patterns. Sports have training books and playbooks. Knitting classes and groups at your favorite yarn shop or conference? Sounds a lot like getting together for practice with the coach. You don't have to explain your boundless interest and passion for knitting as long as grown men are painting their shirtless bodies with team colors. You don't have to explain all the yarn . . . Well, you may have to explain all the yarn, but wouldn't it be easier to explain if there was a closet full of hockey equipment right next to it? I think so too.

The Marathon

This is a long-distance knitting event stressing endurance. Many knitters undertake this sport, though not always intentionally. A marathon may be a planned undertaking, such as the making of an afghan or a sweater for a large friend, but occasionally marathons spring up spontaneously out of other projects. Many a knitter has ended up in an endurance event by accident, when a piece of knitting that was supposed to be simple ends up forcing the knitter to rip back mistakes and knit it again and again and again. This kind of knitting is less like a city marathon or endurance run in which athletes traverse an enormous distance over a long route and more like running laps.

HIGH POINT: Finishing, in any condition.

FLAME OUT: Stuffing the sweater in the back of your closet when, after four goes, the sleeve is still wrong, and pretending to the yarn shop that you have no idea what they are talking about when they ask after it.

The Time Trial

The time trial is the most difficult of all the events, largely because it's usually a combination event. Simply put, knitters must finish a project on a deadline as a gift. By itself, this would be difficult, but this event is almost always combined with other demanding procedures. Its most challenging version takes place at Christmas, when a knitter must finish hats, scarves, and other items for gifts while simultaneously executing tree trimming, cookie baking, entertaining an endless parade of guests, wrapping gifts, and crying into her wool.

HIGH POINT: Finishing everything on your list.

FLAME OUT: Any series of events that ends with a knitter buying desperate and weird gifts at two in the morning at an all-night IGA.

KNITTING SPORTS

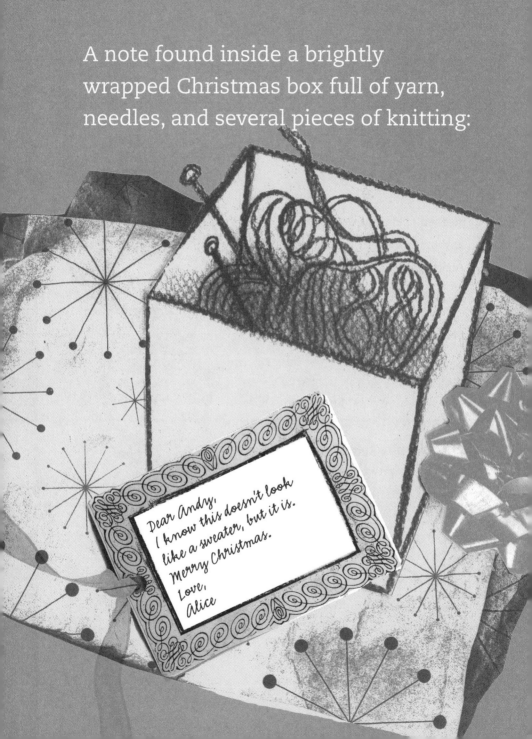

A note found inside a brightly wrapped Christmas box full of yarn, needles, and several pieces of knitting:

Dear Andy,
I know this doesn't look like a sweater, but it is. Merry Christmas.
Love,
Alice

Synchronized Sock Making

This is the simplest of events as far as rules are concerned, but do not let the seemingly uncomplicated rules encourage you. It's difficult. Using regular sock yarn and only their human wits, knitters must come up with a pair of socks that match precisely.

HIGH POINT: Achieving this feat with a ball of self-patterning sock yarn.

FLAME OUT: Two socks that are fraternal rather than identical twins.

Useful Translation

This isn't really working out. This sweater has three arms, but I'm not ready to give up.

Extreme Cast-Off Yarn Challenge

This is everybody's favorite event. It's thrilling just to hear the cast-off surfers tell tall tales of tricky cast-offs executed as they were running out of yarn: "Will there be enough? Whoa, did you see how close that was? There's, like, six feet left! When I was knitting along on the last row, I was just flying, and when I looked over at the yarn I was, like, 'Dude, I don't think I'm gonna make it.' Then I was, like, halfway down the row and I thought, 'Am I gonna make it or am I gonna, like, flame out?' Ya know? So then I thought 'Just go for it. Just try the row, man, just try it!' So I just kept knitting and then it was, like, the end of the last row and that's how much was left, dude. Just feet. It was awesome, it was, like, so close to the edge. Radical."

HIGH POINT: Finishing with only inches of yarn left.

FLAME OUT: Needing to buy and join a whole new skein of yarn to do the last four stitches of the cast-off.

Dangerous words for a knitter on a budget

- **NEW.** Avert your eyes. New yarn to which you have no immunity is very dangerous.

- **SOFT.** Knitters are a tactile people and have been known to buy yarn that they have no pattern or plan for, simply be- cause it's soft.

- **CASHMERE, SILK, GUANACO, YAK, BUFFALO, ANGORA, QUIVIT.** These exotic fibers from rare and spectacular sources are no match for the common knitter. Should a yarn shop owner attempt to show you these, retreat immediately from the store unless you can afford to have an accident.

- **SALE.** Huge amounts of money are spent by knitters who are busy saving money, and the words *discount yarn* are devastating yarn shop weapons.

Don't Say This

Even if you believe it to be true and can probably get a note from a psychiatrist who will appear as a witness in court to back you up, *never* say to a knitter: "You're very obsessed with this string thing."

First of all, my ignorant friend, it's knitting, not a "string thing"; second, that kind of disrespect won't get you a sweater; and finally, we don't think of ourselves as obsessed, but rather as exquisitely focused in a very narrow direction.

CULTURE AND THE ARTS

LIKE PAINTING, LIKE MAKING MUSIC, like dance or poetry, knitting fires the human intellect. I know this is one of the big stumbling blocks for non-knitters when it comes to understanding why knitting excites us, but it's because of its parallels with art and its similarity to other forms of human expression that knitting reaches so many of our spiritual places. It has often been said of knitting that it's a form of meditation, and it's no coincidence that art in all of its forms has often contributed to the spiritual development of the human soul.

Knitting has been called the new yoga, meditation in motion, soothing, relaxing, restful, and a good way to unwind. In history it has been prescribed to cure nervousness, hysteria, and depression in women, and there is evidence in modern science to indicate that knitting lowers your blood pressure, improves hand–eye coordination, evens breathing, reduces tension, and slows your heart rate. One study even found that people who were knitters as young adults had less incidence of Alzheimer's disease as they aged.

All of this is fabulous, of course, and sort of a lie, because knitting is absolutely none of these things when you first start. In fact, a lot of knitters would tell you that the first few times they knit, they learned that this hobby can give you high blood pressure, create anxiety, and cause hysteria.

Though it would appear that when we take up our knitting needles and yarn, it looks like we are doing humble needlework, in reality, knitting is like creating music. Imagine an orchestra beginning to play a symphony. The violins start playing the melody and laying the foundation for the rest of the music. Then the wind instruments join them, playing a counterpoint to the melody and adding another dimension, while the brass instruments play their own separate part. Each of the elements of an orchestra has a role to play and each even has its own sheet music, but in the end, all these parts combine into a whole that wouldn't work without each instrument playing in its own good measure. Painting is the same: The line, the colors, the perspective and form — each of these elements comes together like the instruments in an orchestra to create a piece of art that wouldn't work if any one of the individual elements choked. I'm pretty sure that knitting functions the exact same way.

I know, I know: Until you can find gansey sweaters in the Louvre (where I think there should actually be a Shetland shawl as well), non-knitting people, even knitters themselves, are going to have a really hard time seeing the *Mona Lisa* or

Beethoven's Ninth Symphony in the same light, but stay with me for a minute.

Knitting is made up of parts. Each individual stitch, each singular step, a sleeve, a front, a hood — they all come together in a sweater that won't work unless the knitter sees it as a whole. This is true not just of sweaters. I dare you to try to knit a sock without thinking through the relationship of the gusset to the heel. Without executing both together, the thing wouldn't fit a zucchini, let alone a human foot. Knitting, like music and art, challenges us to see how parts become a whole, and in doing so, it provides many of the same incredible benefits for your brain. The ability to think creatively, contiguously, and linearly . . . knitting challenges our brains and makes us better thinkers.

Knitting is also very approachable. Not everyone can find the beauty in a work of abstract art or an opera, but there is no person alive who can't identify a good hat when she sees one. Knitting holds a special yet common place in the human heart, and that's why, though it's often stunning, it can also drive you right out of your freaking tree. The simple nature of knitting combined with the intense complexity of making it all work together sometimes . . . I bet Beethoven would have loved it.

Good Reading for Knitters

A Good Yarn by Debbie Macomber
A Murderous Yarn by Monica Ferris
A Tale of Two Cities by Charles Dickens
Bag of Bones by Stephen King
D Is for Deadbeat by Sue Grafton
Died in the Wool by Mary Kruger
Jacob's Room by Virginia Woolf
Knit One, Kill Two by Maggie Sefton
Knitting by Anne Bartlett
London Transports by Maeve Binchy
Murder Among Us by Ann Granger
The Miss Marple books by Agatha Christie
The Shop on Blossom Street by Debbie Macomber
The Veiled One by Ruth Rendell

February 11

Dear Marg:

My life this week did not work out. Let's skip the details but agree that if my boss were to discover weeping hives all over his arse and hair growing in huge tufts from underneath all of his nails, I would not think it a sad day but only the beginning of what he deserved . . . but I digress.

My point (my boss's arse aside) is that this week for the first time, I experienced that other dimension of knitting. You know how every time somebody at the yarn shop tells me that they knit to relieve stress, I fall down on the floor and laugh? Today, I finally understand. I totally get it.

This week I was out of my mind at work and my boss was all over me, and for the first time ever I reached for my knitting to try and calm myself. I pulled that blue blanket from my bag, and when my boss asked me what I was doing, I told him I was "just going to do a few rows to take the edge off."

I don't know what he thought. I don't care. Within seconds of picking up my knitting, I felt better. I knit quietly and my mind cleared, my heart slowed. . . . I started feeling much calmer. Even better, my boss chilled out pretty quickly and I think he spoke nicely to me for the rest of the day. I can't tell if the knitting zoned me out just enough that I thought he was nice or if he was actually behaving nicely so that I wouldn't take out the knitting again.

Either way, I'm glad that I've become good enough at this that I can use it to relieve stress instead of to channel it.

Alice

Four Ways
Knitting Is Like Playing the Violin

1. Both knitting and music rely on rows. In knitting, these rows are layers of stitches worked from a chart or pattern; in music, the layers of notes are laid out in sheet music.

2. Both are worked from a chart.

3. Whether you sit down with yarn and needles or violin and bow, it is possible, depending on your mood and competence, to come up with something either wonderful and beautiful or horrific and grating. All you need to do is screw up gauge or play out of tune.

4. When done well and with experience, both knitting and playing the violin look easy. (Knitters and violinists will likely be asked to practice in private when first learning because both knitting and playing can produce foul noise in the early stages.)

Music for Knitting

CDS

More Yarn Will Do the Trick

A CD of songs for textile lovers by Jean Moss and The Purly Kings

Available at www.jeanmoss.com

Wren Ross's Greatest Knits

A CD of songs for knitters by Wren Ross

Available at www.wrenross.com

BANDS (That Aren't about Knitting, but Should Be)

The Cardigans
The Knitters
The Sweater Club
Wool
Needles

ALBUMS (Still Not about Knitting, but Proof of Knitters' Influence)

Tightly Knit (The Climax Blues Band)
Wool (Wool)
Dyed in the Wool (Shannon Wright)
Needles and Pins (The Searchers)
Knitting Needles and Bicycle Bells (Tenement Halls)
Slip, Stitch & Pass (Phish)

And naturally, if this still isn't enough, a knitter would always enjoy any music written for "strings."

RELIGION: IN THE KNITTING BASKET OF GOOD AND EVIL

KNITTING WARMLY WELCOMES and includes all religions, and, as a matter of course, it has has a relationship with almost every faith that knitters come in.

There are many ways in which the citizens of Knitting choose to uphold good in the world through their art and craft. A lovely example is the prayer shawl. In creating this, the knitter dedicates her time and energy to a recipient, making the knitting of a shawl a prayerful act. Such a shawl is meant to carry the prayers or good wishes of the knitter to the intended and is meant to comfort the one needing its warmth, offering the knitter's cherishing and love. Regardless of faith (or lack thereof), all knitters are familiar with this concept, even if they don't formalize the idea. We've all thought fondly of someone as we knit something for him or her. Perhaps we hoped that the steps someone took in the socks we knit would carry them to happy places, or maybe we knit firm hope into each small stitch of a baby blanket to ensure that with our action, it would surround a happy and healthy infant. We've made people who are sad something beautiful to help them feel better, we've brought someone who's ill something soft to nourish her while she heals, and we've given those who journey something to carry with them as they travel. We've all worried and worked concern into the stitches of an item, and even if we don't formally pray while we do it, the human kindness and the intention to heal hurts are equal to prayer. Knits can carry hope and help.

There's another side to this coin, though — a darker side. What of those knits that you hated? You know the ones: knits that were frustration incarnate; knits with black, black souls that cared nothing for your happiness or well-being or that of anyone else; projects that returned the favor of the love you poured into them by reducing you to tears and impelling you to fling them around the room, trailing ends of renegade yarn and shouting uncivilized language. What is to be said of the spiritual nature of these beasts?

I once worked on a pair of mittens so full of disaster that by the time I was done knitting them, I could have just as easily snipped them into a thousand pieces and eaten them as worn them or given them to someone. The pattern was wrong, then the gauge was wrong, then I made a mistake that meant ripping back. On the second go, I knit with the tail instead of the working yarn on the second round and had to have a do-over again. On the third try, I misplaced one of my double-pointed needles and had to buy another set, and on the fourth try I used the wrong shade of blue for half of the chart. By the time I finished them, these mittens had absorbed more poor attitude and hostility than a high school teacher. If we believe that knitting absorbs our goodwill, can't it also absorb the opposite?

I did end up giving away those mittens, partly because Christmas is a desperate, desperate time and partly because it seemed to me that no matter what the mojo on those things had been while I was knitting them, when they were done, I forgave them everything. They were soft and beautiful and I was proud, and the person I gave them to never complained that they burned her hands or gave her a rash or that she had terrible nightmares of evil sheep and pointed sticks on the days when she wore them.

The experience did leave me wondering, though: Can knitting indeed be turned to the dark side? If you can fill a knit with love, can the reverse be true? Is it possible for knitting to be plied and twisted into something vengeful or evil? Could knitting, in the wrong hands, be a spiritual weapon?

Madame Defarge

Madame Defarge was a knitter who managed to use her knitting for evil. (She was also fictional, starring as the symbol of the cruelty and chaos of the French Revolution in Charles Dickens's *A Tale of Two Cities*, so we don't know if anyone has ever really used knitting for evil.) Throughout the book, we see Madame Defarge knitting, but later we learn that although it looks as though she's simply knitting, she's actually creating a register of the names of all of those whom the Revolutionaries believe must die for the cause. Because keeping a written register would be dangerous and could incriminate her cohorts, Madame Defarge has come up with the idea of using her stitches as a code, thereby turning her knitting into a hit list.

"Are you sure," asked Jacques Two, of Defarge, "that no embarrassment can arise from our manner of keeping the register? Without doubt it is safe, for no one beyond ourselves can decipher it; but shall we always be able to decipher it — or, I ought to say, will she?"

"Jacques," returned Defarge, drawing himself up, "if madame my wife undertook to keep the register in her memory alone, she would not lose a word of it — not a syllable of it. Knitted, in her own stitches and her own symbols, it will always be as plain to her as the sun. Confide in Madame Defarge. It would be easier for the weakest poltroon that lives to erase himself from existence than to erase one letter of his name or crimes from the knitted register of Madame Defarge."

Useful Translation

I'm doing my knitting work.

I'm doing the productive activity with which I like to fill my idle time. (Many people in some parts of the eastern United States who don't knit and don't plan on learning use these words. They don't have anything at all to do with knitting. Knitters should be warned that if they hear someone say this phrase and then rush excitedly to this person's home, yarn in tow, they are just as likely to find someone refinishing a chair or weeding the garden as knitting. Try not to look too disappointed.)

Five Things
You Won't Hear a Knitter Say

1. I'm just bored stupid. Can anyone think of something to do?

2. Aren't moths pretty?

3. Cashmere is so overrated.

4. No, I don't want to go to the yarn shop.

5. You're right. These hand-knit socks are exactly like the ones from Wal-Mart.

March 6

Dear . . . what? Dear Diary? Dear Knitter?

I feel ridiculous. I haven't written in a diary since I was seventeen years old (all that teen angst), but now I find that some of the things I write about knitting I wouldn't want to tell anyone, so Dear Diary it is.

The thing is, **I love knitting.**

There. I said it. I almost wrote "don't tell anyone" after it, but I guess if I'm not sending this to anyone, there's no point in trying to keep it a secret. Anyway, everyone can probably tell by the way I spend all my time. I feel as though I've unlocked a secret door. I knit at night. I knit in the daytime. I swear that I'm going to knit "just one more row" and then two hours slip by. I get in a quick row before my coffee in the morning and I pore over pattern books and magazines. I listen intently when people talk about knitting, I suddenly notice sweaters in movies, and last night I did something crazy.

I was shopping for fall clothes at a store that I like and I tried on a fabulous sweater. It fit like a million bucks: The ribbing was the right length, the bust was perfect, the neckline hung exactly right . . . it was a great sweater. These days, though, I'm not the sort of person who will buy a sweater. The old Alice, the "before knitting" Alice would have snapped up that sweater in a heartbeat. But the new Alice,

Knitter Alice . . .

I took my tape measure out of my purse. (There's something right there: The old Alice didn't carry a tape measure, but the new Alice has one in her purse with her knitting.) I laid the sweater on the table in the store, glanced around surreptitiously to see if anyone was watching, smoothed it, and measured it. I measured the bust, I measured the sleeves, I measured the length and how deep the armholes were, and I wrote it all down on the back of an envelope in my bag. I was just making a note about the neckline when Andy came in and saw me.

"Why don't you try it on to see if it fits?" he said (probably wondering when I had lost my stinking mind, something he's likely been pondering since he found the mohair in the trunk of the car). "Weren't you saying you needed a sweater?"

"I do need a new sweater," I said, folding the sweater and leaving it on the table, "and I did try it on," I said as I put the envelope and tape measure back in my purse. "It's going to be perfect."

I ignored the way he looked at me (as though I had three freaking eyes or something) as we left the store — and the sweater.

My next sweater is going to fit perfectly. This is what I've become. The new Alice. Alice the sweater spy.

Alice

"Traveling tends to magnify all human emotions."

— Peter Høeg

EXTENDING YOUR STAY

VISITORS TO KNITTING should be aware that once they spend some time there, even though they plan on a short stay, it may be impossible to leave. Initially, it was thought that this inability to leave was due to high concentrations of yarn fumes, but this theory was shattered when knitters were discovered working with wire, string, and other materials that give off no particular odors. It should be noted that the effects of knitting are common — and are therefore considered normal — in the land of Knitting. They are now considered an environmental risk of the land itself, sort of like getting a sunburn in the Bahamas.

Personality changes indicating a resident's inability to leave Knitting are:

- **Vague dishonesty or a predilection to tell "white lies."** For example, knitters may claim that they don't want to go to a movie when they would actually love to see a movie but don't want to sit in a dark space where they can't see to knit.

- **Development of patience.** Previously impatient types suddenly may not mind waiting for appointments, taking long car trips, or sitting through grade school concerts of unbelievable length as long as they are not separated from their knitting during this time. (Removal of knitting is not recommended; doing so will cause their original impatience to return with increased force and possibly . . . violence.)

- **Tolerance.** Residents of Knitting find it increasingly easy to deal with annoying people. They simply take out their knitting and pretend to listen.

TRAVEL TIP

The more remotely you travel, the more yarn you should take. You don't want to end up knitting seaweed on a beach vacation because you ran out of the real stuff.

Knitting Traveling Projects

If you're going to be a knitter about town or a knitter out of town, then the size and type of your project should relate to where you're going and how you're going to get there. I've learned the hard way that not all projects travel well — and if you don't believe me, just imagine a summer vacation when all you've brought to knit is an afghan. Spend three hours in the blazing sun with that much wool spread on your lap and you'll see where I'm going with this. It's like a vacation in Hades.

Examples of Reasonable Packing according to Type of Trip

- For a one-week trip by plane to Hawaii: A minimum of three projects — one small project that fits in your carry-on bag; one project (preferably not wool or white) for the beach; and one project (your choice) for dining, drinking, and relaxing indoors.
- For a three-day road trip: Three days is a lot of knitting time, so pack at least three generous projects — one on larger needles, one on smaller needles, and one garter-stitch project for when the hundreds of miles of I-75 start to wear on you a little. If you have to split the driving, bring the same amount. You never know when you'll need extra knitting. If you bring

a project that requires you to read a chart, bring another that has no chart. Chart- and pattern-reading in the car makes some knitters carsick (and sand and sunscreen aren't the only things that are hard to get out of mohair, if you catch my meaning).

TRAVEL TIP

Road trips demand special planning, because they provide many consecutive hours of knitting time. To avoid hand strain or injury, take breaks often, stretch your hands, and mix up the projects according to needle type (circular or straight) and gauge (heavy yarn or fine yarn). Put all of your yarn and projects into a bag by your feet so you don't have to pull over frequently and rummage through the trunk. Trunk rummaging does not go over well with travel companions interested in "making good time."

Three Ways
to Get More Knitting Time on a Road Trip

1. **"Forget" your glasses** so you won't be asked to drive. (*Note:* This won't work if you need your glasses to knit.)

2. **As you drive, talk incessantly about knitting.** Tell your carmates that you have to either knit or talk about it. Their choice will not surprise you.

3. **Sing the Willie Nelson song** "On the Road Again" at top volume any time you are behind the wheel. It's a good bet you'll have more knitting time in short order.

Ten Commandments
for the Traveling Knitter

1 Thou shalt not be concerned that you have packed more yarn, patterns, reference books, and needles than clothing. You can wear the same clothes twice, but when a project is finished, it's done.

2 Thou shalt forgive those who point out to you that you cannot knit up twelve skeins of yarn in a twelve-hour road trip. They know not the fear of running out.

3 Thou shalt feel just fine about taking five hours to decide what knitting to bring with you but only five minutes to choose your clothing. You're going to spend more time admiring your knitting.

4 Thou shalt investigate the local embassies and consulates of Knitting wherever you travel. You know not what wonders faraway yarn shops and guilds have in store for you.

5 Should thy mate sigh when you reveal that your vacation plans fall on the same route as a dozen yarn shops, you shall distract him with chocolate and remind him that his interest in obtaining a silver spoon from all fifty U.S. states or locating new golf courses is similarly suspect and just as time- and gas-consuming

6 Thou shalt pack more than one
project for your vacation. You may
tire of the one you are planning on knitting.
Indeed, no one has ever suffered harm by bringing
four or more projects on one trip.

7 Thou shalt feel no guilt when you purchase souvenir yarn.
It is more useful than postcards and less silly than another
T-shirt.

8 So as to better spread the word of knitting, thou shalt explain with enthusiasm and generosity when, as you travel,
someone asks you about your knitting.

9 Thou shalt approach without fear other knitters you meet
while traveling. You have a great deal in common, even if it
may not seem that way at first.

10 Thou shalt allow your mate to believe it is a complete coincidence that the family lunch stop is eerily close to the only
yarn shop within a thousand miles. Only you will know it is
the by-product of several hours spent with a map; the Yellow Pages; and a considerable amount of detailed research,
e-mails, and telephone calls.

Knitters in the Air

I travel a lot, and for a long time I kept wondering why I always had my suitcase searched. I'm a nice little Canadian with no record of criminal activity and I don't think my mother has written to any official with her suspicions that I may not be normal, so I could not figure out why my suitcase always came back to me with the note: "We ruffled through your delicates. Hope you don't mind." I was pondering this question one day as I took my swift and ball winder out of my suitcase and tried desperately to think of what on earth could be so suspicious about me that my suitcase was searched almost every time I came within ten feet of an airport.

It was only as I clamped the swift to the hotel-room bedside table (using a pair of clean underpants to pad the table so that the clamp wouldn't damage it) and opened out its umbrella-like metal structure that it occurred to me that the swift might look a tiny bit weird on X-ray. I bet the ball winder wasn't helping, either. Since I started leaving my swift and ball winder at home and relying on local yarn shops in the places where I'm visiting to do my winding for me, I swear that I'm searched about a third of the time.

TRAVEL TIP

Sunscreen totally stains yarn, and sand never really comes out of it.

Air-Travel Packing Tips

As difficult as it may be for knitters to believe, common knitter stuff is not frequently carried by traveling non-knitters. For the non-knitter responsible for screening your bag at the airport, swifts, ball winders, needles (circular, straight, and double-pointed), darning needles, scissors, stitch holders, cable needles, gauges, and metal tape measures can set off alarm bells (especially when they appear together in one suitcase). Given that our aim of having one knitter stationed at each X-ray machine in every airport in the world is progressing slowly, the following tips may help you and your luggage clear security more quickly.

- **As often as possible, avoid taking any of the aforementioned items in your carry-on bag.** Needles are usually allowed, but the swift is going to be very hard (though not impossible) to explain.

- **Put your yarn in a zip-top baggie.** It helps to keep it from rolling around and upsetting security people, who don't like being tied up.

- **Put on top of the contents of your luggage any items (such as a metal swift) that may look unusual on X-ray.** It might save your bag from being entirely rifled if they can find the weird stuff straightaway.

What Can You Take on a Plane?

Yes

- **Knitting needles.** This will vary from airline to airline. Most carriers in Canada and the United States do not restrict knitting needles at all, but some European carriers are still quite fussy. Your chances are improved by carrying wooden circulars or bamboo double-pointed needles instead of long metal straights.
- **Yarn**
- **Cable needles**
- **A cloth tape measure**
- **Patterns**
- **Ball winders.** This is not recommended, though. It weirds people out when you wind wool on flights. Besides, there's no place to put the swift.
- **Swifts (see above)**

No

- **Scissors**
- **Darning or sewing needles**
- **A metal tape measure**
- **Any kind of yarn cutter, including the pendent ones with a sharp wheel inside**

Note: Although knitting needles are "allowed items" under both Canadian and U.S. security guidelines, even in these countries all airlines reserve the right to refuse to allow you to carry them on board. It doesn't happen much, but the occasional nervous security officer will tell you that you can't bring them on the plane, and she's within her rights to do so. Each security officer makes her own decisions. If you are told you may not bring needles on board, pointing out that you are more dangerous without your knitting than you are with it (no matter how true this is) will not help and is definitely not advised. For the record, pointing out all the other stuff you're carrying that could be just as dangerous as knitting needles (like your pen) is really, really not advised.

DESPERATION TIP

No matter how much it bothers you that pencils (long, pointy wooden sticks) are allowed on all flights but knitting needles (long, pointy wooden sticks) are occasionally refused, you can turn this to your advantage. Knit with pencils. You can get a big chunk of a scarf done on a flight. (Use an elastic on the eraser to keep the stitches from falling off the "needles.")

Vacations

For knitters, the truth about vacations is that they are never what you expect at all. Either you end up knitting way, way more than you thought you would or way, way less. Sadly, because the land of Knitting can have an unpredictable yarn supply, you must always pack for the former situation. A vacation with tons of time to knit and no yarn is a nightmare no knitter wants to face, and frankly, most of us are willing to carry a second suitcase to avoid it.

April 2

Sarah,

I'm home safe and sound, though I barely escaped the airport with my yarn intact.

Remember how you laughed at how much yarn I was trying to fit in my suitcase for the plane ride home? (Even I felt like I might have too much when you had to sit on the case to get the zipper closed.) Well, you won't believe what happened: My suitcase was selected for a search and after that, I was sent over to some part of customs. (I swear, next time I'm putting all of my underpants in Ziplocks — I'm so creeped out.)

As I walked there, dragging this huge suitcase of yarn behind me, I tried to figure out why I could possibly be in trouble. At customs they lifted my suitcase on to a table, opened it, and told me I was being assessed duty charges.

"Duty? On what?"

The lady pointed at all of my yarn and told me that from the amount I was bringing back, it was clear that I was importing yarn for resale because nobody could purchase that much yarn for personal use.

Once I convinced her that it was indeed all for me — it helped that I had three works in progress in my bag and a sock in my purse — they thought it was funny, but for a minute there I wondered if I had really gone over the top with the stash thing.

Love,

Alice

P.S. Thanks for mailing the yarn that wouldn't fit in the suitcase. I'll let you know when it gets here.

"A journey of a thousand miles must begin with a single step."

— **Lao-tzu**

Nancy Bush

Nancy Bush lives in Utah and is a respected member of Knitting's foreign service. In addition to her own formidable knitting skills and prolific book production, Nancy works to teach and record the varied and gripping approaches to knitting all over the world. She travels extensively and her greatest gift to knitting is likely her commitment to understanding, translating, and recording the folk knitting of Estonia. Few of us will ever have a chance to travel there, but thanks to Nancy, we can all appreciate and learn the traditional skills of Estonian knitters.

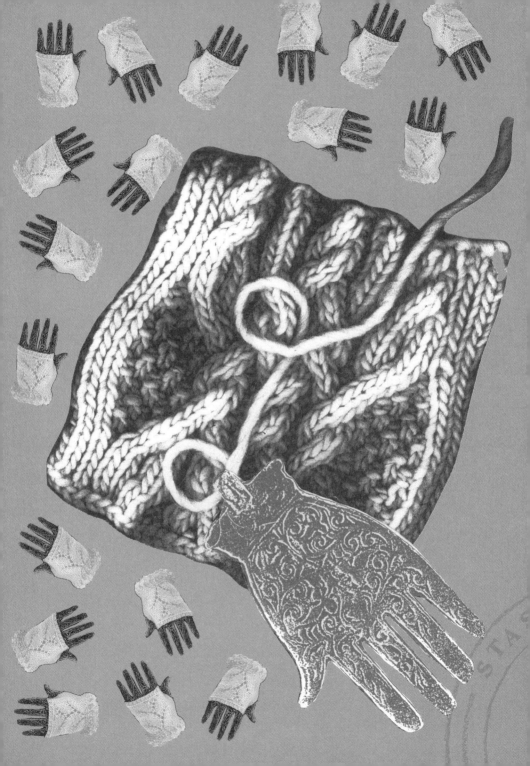

BELIEFS
AND CUSTOMS

JUST AS IN SOUTH AMERICA some people believe in the evil eye or in China people may worry about keeping turtles as pets (lest they slow down their business), people in the land of Knitting have their own beliefs, superstitions, and customs. One of these suggests that a master knitter place knitting needles in the hands of a baby to make sure the infant will pick up the practice. Another says that bad luck can be averted by avoiding stabbing needles through yarn. (Avoiding stabbing anything seems wise, really.) Another belief tells that to avoid damaging a friendship (or a friend), you should never hand knitting needles to anyone point first. It seems that superstitions abound in knitting, and some of them are complex.

The Ritual of the Swatch

Technically speaking, a swatch is a small sample of knitting executed before the actual knitting of a garment. Knitters are admonished to swatch for the purpose of ascertaining their gauge. In this way, they can make sure their gauge is accurate and they can determine if the yarn and needles are going to perform in the expected manner. We are told that if we make swatches, wash, and measure them, they will tell us much of what's in store in the knitting ahead. The general idea is that swatches are a window into the future; they predict the shape of things to come.

This is a lie. It doesn't take long for most knitters to catch on to the fact that swatches guarantee little. The astute among us, having faithfully knit swatches, washed them, measured our gauge from them, then reverently set them at our side while we knit a sweater that ended up resembling the gauge swatch exactly the way that socks resemble Brie, have caught on to the mysteries and cruelties of gauge.

Knitting science tells us that gauge swatches are occasionally (if we take the word *occasionally* to mean "almost always") unreliable because there are too many variables involved in knitting: An entire sweater has a weight that can pull the gauge out of whack; subtle differences that can't be seen in a small swatch become obvious in an entire knitted shawl; and occasionally (again, meaning "almost always") the stalwart knitter herself is blamed for measuring unreliably or failing to count stitches properly during the critical gauge assessment phase.

Longtime residents of Knitting, however, have an explanation for why we knit swatches (given that the "useful" explanation clearly falls down when the thing doesn't work): They know that we knit them as offerings to the knitting fates. Like bowls of water offered to Buddha; money placed on the church plate on Sunday; burnt offerings in an ancient Jewish temple; flowers for the Hindu god Vishnu; and Zakat, the Muslim practice of giving alms, knitting a swatch can be seen as a sacrifice to the muses of knitting. In creating them, we offer up time and yarn and then hope that the disaster set to befall us as we knit will be offset by this offering of squares of trial knitting. We keep knitting swatches because our faith as knitters demands that we believe in this ritual.

It somehow seems that these swatches, dreams of knitting that we create and set beside us while we begin a project, can actually make a difference to the outcome of our knitting — and every once in a while, stunningly, whether by luck, talent, or chance, gauge swatches actually work. In these instances, our faith in knitting them is entirely restored and all the times they screwed us over are forgotten.

I'm betting, though, that more than one knitter has thought about burning a whack of gauge swatches — especially the ones that ended up being useless squares of wasted time and wool.

In actuality, gauge is influenced by needle size, yarn thickness, and how loosely or tightly you're knitting. If you're having a gauge difficulty, you're having difficulty with one of these three elements, and changing one or more of them should fix the problem. As far as is known, changing your attitude or choice of swear words or locking yourself in the basement with a voodoo doll of the sweater's designer does little but make you feel better.

April 20

Dear Designer,

This is a note of apology for my rather hasty (and somewhat rude) e-mail of late last night. I blame sweater failure and the crushing weight of dashed hopes. My behavior was unbecoming to a knitter. I hope you can forgive me for my irrational and hostile tone and that I will still be permitted (when I take up knitting again; I'm a little off it right this minute) to purchase your patterns.

Now that I've had some sleep and coffee, I realize that I was out of line when I called your pattern "an obvious attack on knitters everywhere" and I beg your forgiveness. In the cold, hard light of day I know that if I make an abomination of your pattern, it is hardly your fault, but late last night, when I triumphantly sewed the last seam and finally slipped on my beautiful finished sweater only to realize that it wouldn't fit me, I sort of came undone.

Perhaps I would not have reacted so strongly if the sweater simply wasn't my size. It is the fact that it isn't the size of any human who has ever walked this earth that caused me to lose my composure. Clearly, given that the sleeves are long enough that I can flag down freaking SPACECRAFT by flapping them, we may presume that I have experienced some difficulty with my gauge, which is not at all your fault, and my suggestion that you were to blame and should stick anything anywhere at all was inappropriate.

I cannot apologize enough for the things I said about your motivation and intention for my sanity. I feel particularly bad about calling into question the decency of your mother. I'm sure she's lovely.

That said, may I suggest, with all humble respect,

that you make one minor change in the pattern? You certainly don't owe me anything after the string of particularly demeaning expletives contained in the greeting of my regrettable letter last evening, but I request that you and all designers immediately cease implying to knitters everywhere that if they knit a swatch, get gauge, and then knit the sweater in that gauge, the sweater will be a predictable size. As near as I can tell, there is really no more than a 50/50 chance of this.

Following your instructions, I did a swatch and I did get gauge. Then, despite being a good person who takes direction well, I did not get a sweater of the size you claimed I would. It's time to stop the charade and come clean on the element of chance in knitting. The existence of gauge swatches and your suggestion that knitting them is a magic pathway to sweaters you can actually wear are an insult to every knitter who ever got gauge and then got a sleeveless dress instead of a tank top.

Many thanks, and again, sincerest apologies,

Alice

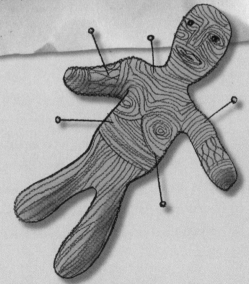

I HAVE A FRIEND who gets all of the fashion magazines. I don't. I'm short, my arse never fits into pants properly, my hair has its own agenda, and I own only two pairs of shoes. These magazines are not for me. My friend, however, loves them and finds them intriguing; she really thinks it's helpful to find out that all of her clothes from last year are garbage this year. She scans the magazines, carefully noting what's hip and what's hot. I think it's a waste of knitting time.

Awhile ago, one magazine she was looking at showed pictures of celebrities who wore their hair the same way and included a big article on how this was really the style of the moment. My friend looked at the celebrities and the hairstyles and said, "I'm going to hate wearing my hair like that." I was stunned. If you hate the hairstyle, why would you wear it? "It's in," she said. "Bangs are out. I can't go around with bangs. Bangs are last year." She sighed deeply, looked at the magazine again, and said, "It's peer pressure. I like to be stylish and this is the style. You know what it's like." Then we both laughed. My own style is a sort of a post-apocalyptic "I spend all my money on yarn" and "I'm too busy knitting to apply lipstick" look, and I'm the last person in the world who would fold to peer pressure or "know what it's like".

Or so I thought. One day, I was tidying up the stash a bit and ran into a shawl that has been on needles for the better part of two years. From time to time, I take it out and work on it a little, but to be completely fair, it holds absolutely no charm for me. I don't like the yarn and never did. Then I pulled out a sweater, similarly abandoned, and realized I didn't like it either. Then there was that funny-colored sock yarn, the silk that was an absolutely inexplicable shade of beige that reminds me of old moths. There were others, but I don't think I need to lower myself by telling you exactly how many.

I don't understand this. I should love all my projects. I chose the yarn and bought it, I cast them on. Everything I knit and everything in my stash should be right up my alley. We can all understand that there are projects or yarn that you start out loving but come to hate over time, and then there's the stuff that you used to adore but have since outgrown — but yarn and projects you actively dislike? What was I doing with this junk?

Right then the whole thing hit me like a ton of bricks. I thought about my hairstyle friend and I got it. *She's fallen for a fashion trick, I fell for a yarn trick. I bought most of the yarn because I was with a bunch of other knitters and it was on sale.* My friends were all excited and I got excited and eventually I'm standing here holding a project that I don't like and won't ever finish, and every time I try to explain how I came to have thirty-four skeins of bubblegum-colored cotton or why I'm avoiding a powder blue shawl, everything I say starts sounding like it did when I was a teenager: "But Mum, everybody was doing it!"

Peer pressure is a deadly force in knitting. It has the ability to make you believe that you should buy the same yarn as everybody else just because it's 50 percent off. Peer pressure can make you knit socks you think are dumb and peer pressure can have you finishing off a sweater that's totally ridiculous for your figure. Stay strong, be tough, be true to yourself, and don't impulsively buy yarn while under the influence of other knitters.

Above all, when it comes to buying yarn , starting projects, or getting bangs, ask yourself: If everybody jumped off a bridge, would I do it?

A Knitter Has Cast Off

It is terrible and sad when a knitter passes, but the families and friends of those left behind after she has gone to the great big yarn shop in the sky have a remarkable comfort left them: the things their knitter made. Each of these items is not just a remembrance but something far more incredible. The hats, scarves, sweaters, and shawls that your knitter leaves you when she dies are not just tangible proof of her love for you; they also represent big chunks of her time.

An afghan only looks like an afghan. In reality, it is something close to a hundred hours of your knitter's life — time she spent on you when she could have been doing anything else. It is proof of a portion of her life spent sitting — maybe even sitting with you — and happily working the thousands of stitches that you now have, each one recording a moment of your knitter's life as surely as a camera. Long after your knitter is no longer with you, you can hold the things she created and you can feel the time, hours of your knitter's life, that she wanted you to have, all disguised as a soft blue hat. I think about this sometimes when

I'm knitting: I'm leaving a legacy of work and time. In these objects I'm leaving things my descendants will look at generations from now and that will hold who I was and what I did while I was here. When I think about this, I'm really touched. Then I realize that's a pretty good motivator to knit better stuff.

What to Do with a Dead Knitter's Stash

It may seem harsh to say so, but the sad truth is that almost all knitters will die someday, and most of them are going to leave behind a stash the size of a small country's gross domestic product. Their friends and families are going to wonder what to do with all of that wool. If you're like me, then you probably can't stand the idea that all of your stash will be sold at a garage sale or thrown into bags in the garage or basement, waiting to wither and become moth food. You're going to need a posthumous yarn plan.

Write a yarn will. Your family will be surprised to see it among your effects, because no matter how cheerfully or reverently a family takes to the stash, they never really understand its deeply personal nature and dollar value. (You can't blame them for this; it's in a knitter's best interest to be exceedingly vague about the financial investment in her stash as long as she is alive.) Tell your family and the executor of the will the value of the stash and charge them with giving the yarn to the knitters named. When writing the will, note that this is a chance to right wrongs and correct past failings. Remember last year when you were in the yarn shop and Sue said she liked that red yarn and then (right after you touched it) you took leave of every shred of decency you had and bought it all while she was in the ladies room? Assuming Sue outlives you, you can make up for that.

Designate recipients. When I was a little girl, my mum and I visited my great-aunt Naomi. While we were there, my mother complimented a beautiful footstool in the living room, and without missing a beat, Auntie Omi flipped it over. On the bottom of the stool was a piece of masking tape, and on the tape was written BARB. "Sorry, dear," Omi said regretfully, "that's already taken. How about this nice clock?" and she turned over the mantel clock to reveal a blank piece of tape. You can do the same thing with the stash. Store everything in a zip-top bag (I love those things) and write on the label: "Sue: Regrets for telling you it was too scratchy to buy and then going back to get it myself. Enjoy."

Donate it to a thrift shop. Not every knitter is organized enough to pull off a will or a labeled stash. Some knitters even die suddenly, mid-project. For knitters who die intestate, this is an excellent method of stash dispersal. When I was a young mother, I didn't have any money . . . or at least no yarn money once I bought food. As a result, I used to haunt thrift stores looking for sweaters I could unravel for the wool and I lurked near the craft aisle, hoping a ball of yarn would turn up. Again and again, all that ever arrived were Christmas-colored dishcloth cotton (complete with the silver sparkles) and half skeins of acid-yellow polyester. It was heartbreaking (as were the kids' sweaters that I made from the stuff; I'll end up paying for their therapy for those). If I'd ever found anything truly nice there, I think I would have cried. When I go, the stash is going to that store, and some young mother with no money, excellent taste, and a toddler in an expertly cabled puce polyester cardigan is going to have a really, really great day.

Scrambles. There was a tradition where I grew up in Toronto, though I don't know if it spread out of my city or province: A kid on a run of good fortune would swagger into the schoolyard, gather a crowd around him, and then shout at the top of his lungs "SCRAMBLES!" while tossing in the air a handful of candy or gum or sparklers . . . whatever he felt moved to pass along. We'd all scramble, swarming around our benefactor, each one of us grabbing for whatever had been tossed that day. It was barbaric, but it had a certain childish fairness to it. It was part skill and part luck, and it meant that nobody had to choose favorites when giving out gum. In my wildest dreams I imagine the knitterly version of this, where the widow of a knitter simply walks into a knitting guild meeting with a huge box (or ten boxes) containing the dead knitter's stash, takes a deep breath, and yells "SCRAMBLES!" at the top of her lungs.

Making a Traveler's Life Afghan

This is one of my favorite projects and one that can reflect a
knitter's journey as well as any scrapbook or postcard collection.
It was inspired by a quilt I had as a little girl made of the leftover scraps of fabric from the clothes my grandmother sewed.
There was a square that was a piece of my mother's favorite
nightie, a square of an uncle's flannel shirt, bits of a summer
sundress and a soft bedsheet. Our lives and stories about what
people did and where they went in the clothes made from those
fabrics were laid out in bits and pieces and backed with pink
cotton, and I loved it. This knitting project serves the same purpose: It uses the leftovers of projects gone by (or as they go by,
my personal choice) to work a traveler's afghan.

STEP 1: Look at your stash and your leftovers. Is the yarn
mostly fingering weight? Mostly chunky? Think a little bit about
the average thickness of the yarn you like to use. Don't worry if
you have a little bit of everything. That's healthy. Just determine
what you think is the average thickness of the yarn in the stash.

STEP 2: Go get a nice, long circular needle that matches the
thickness of the yarn you love the most. When I do this, I always
end up with a US 8 (5 mm) needle.

STEP 3: Leaving a long end (at least six inches) and using leftovers or stash yarn that matches your needle size (more or less;
I promise it isn't going to matter much), cast on a reasonable

number of stitches for the width of an afghan.

Afghans vary in size a whole lot; any length from forty inches to your wingspan (your height is the same as your wingspan) is going to work. If you're feeling as though you'd like more precision, this formula works:

Your expected number of stitches per inch × how many inches long you would like the afghan to be = the number of stitches to cast on.

STEP 4: Start knitting every stitch, every row. Each time you get to the end of a row, cut the yarn, leaving about six inches, and start another row. Leave a six-inch tail at the end of each row, and change colors and yarn types often. If your new yarn isn't as thick as your average — say you've got a fingering weight instead of the average worsted — hold two strands together, or don't and let the chips fall where they may. The beauty of this afghan is that as long as you keep mixing it up every row or so, it works no matter what your gauge on any individual row.

Note: If you start this afghan and suddenly realize that you just don't have it in you to finish it (it happens to the best of us; afghans are big), you can cast off while it's still a narrow strip and have a really cool scarf.

STEP 5: When the afghan is the desired length, cast off, then create fringe: In groups of five to ten ends, tie into knots the yarn tails at each end of your work. When you have all of them tied in bunches, trim the fringe to a length you like. Congratulate yourself and lay out the afghan in a place where everyone will ask about it.

This pattern has only three rules:

1 Cut the yarn at the end of each row and leave long ends or your fringe won't work. (If you are anti-fringe, you may weave in all of these ends, but it's a prospect too horrible for me to contemplate.)

2 Change yarn often. You may work several rows with the same yarn, but if it's very different in gauge from the next yarn in the queue, the change may be obvious. Mixing it up lets you do as you please, because it's the average gauge that matters, not the gauge of any particular row.

3 Keep the majority of the yarn (or combination of yarns) — at least 50 percent — appropriate to your needle size. If you don't, the thing just won't hang together, structure-wise.

I dream of an afghan worked like this with strands of lace-weight held with fingering, with mohair next to worsted, with a little silk cozying up to plain old wool . . . each of them the leftovers from a project that I completed. I imagine adding to it a row at a time over a whole lifetime of knitting, and I imagine how this afghan would become a wonderful souvenir of all the places I visited and everything I learned.

Note: This project doesn't have to be an afghan. A baby blanket would be less of a commitment (though babies do have an annoying tendency to suck on fringe), and a shawl would be brilliant: Either cast on enough for your wingspan and go to town or begin at the point of the shawl by casting on a single stitch, then increase one stitch at the beginning of every row until your triangle is big enough. Observe the three rules and it will be perfect.

"Certainly,
travel is more
than the seeing of sights;
it is a change that goes on,
deep and permanent, in
the ideas of living."

— **Miriam Beard**

BEING HOME, WHEREVER HOME IS

ALL JOURNEYS, even those to the land of Knitting, must eventually come to an end, but those who travel to Knitting seldom come back. Every journey is supposed to end with coming home — that's the way it works, right? You pack your bags, you go to see something new, and then you come home and pick up where you left off.

Knitting is not like that. Knitting, done right with passion and with the right people, can transform lives, open doors, and teach you new things. Knitting becomes a place you carry with you. Knitting becomes a place that is everywhere you go. Knitting becomes home and is every bit as transformative as any other journey of learning. Knitting offers prizes to those who choose to live within it.

May 1

Dear Marg,

Andy's sweater is finished. It's soft and blue and I don't think anyone has ever knit anything better. I think this despite its uneven arms and crooked seams and even though you couldn't get two bucks for it at a thrift shop. Somehow, when I laid it out, I felt so smart and productive that, honestly, I wanted to show this sweater to strangers on the street. (It is a testament to my self-improvement program that I did not.)

I know that some of the stuff I've knit might be better than this (toward the end of that slipper jag I was banging out some pretty perfect slippers), but this is my first real (finished) sweater, and sweaters aren't just knitting — they're clothes. This here sweater is a Genuine Real Garment. A couple of hundred years ago this would have been the only way my husband could get a sweater and it would have been my responsibility to knit for my whole family . . . they would have needed me to do it to keep them warm. It's good that time marches on, because this project took five months longer than I predicted and if Andy couldn't have picked up a sweater from a store in the meantime, he surely would have succumbed to exposure. Thank goodness we don't have kids. I can only imagine the dire consequences of being a slacker knitter who fails to finish a baby blanket.

I looked at it on the bed when it was done and I imagined Andy coming home and seeing it and realizing — at least, I hope he does — what this really is, what this means. I hope he gets that I've made him a piece of magic. It started out as string and it ended up as clothes and the only things in the world that moved it from one state to the other were the wits, intelligence, and time of a woman who loves him. It's a miracle.

It's been only a year or so since I saw all you knitters in the bookshop and ~~stalked you~~ found out more about knitting.

You know, if you had walked up to me and told me the truth about knitting that day, I would have tried to have you committed. I know this because I've tried to tell people the truth about knitting since then and they all look at me like I'm a few sheep short of a flock. I try to tell them that knitting is endlessly interesting. I try to tell them that it's the only thing I've ever done that's as interesting or as mundane as I need it to be; that when I do it, it's the only time in my life that I feel as though I'm performing magic; and that it's made me a smarter person. I tell them I've learned to think in straighter lines; I tell them I've learned persistence and patience; and I tell them (this may be where I lose them) that yarn, wool, and anything like them are truly emotionally fulfilling to collect. (I tried to tell this to a guy who collects spoons. He laughed at me, and it took everything that I had in me not to shriek after him: "SPOONS, my friend . . . SPOONS are what you collect! Cutlery collectors don't get to say anything about yarn collectors!") Finally, I tell them that what I like best about knitting is Knitters, and that I aspire to be one someday . . . a Knitter with a capital K.

For now, I'm off to find something new to knit, because it's been twenty-five minutes since I finished Andy's sweater and I've got itchy fingers. It's funny: You'd think that looking at that sweater of his would make me feel most like a Knitter, but it's when I have nothing to knit that it really hits me that I've adopted knitting as a lifestyle. What did I do before knitting? Did I really just sit? When I took the bus, did I just sit on the bus? How did I wait in lines? How on earth did I spend the twenty minutes I waited to see the accountant? What did I do while I watched TV? When I think about all the time I spent until now just sitting . . . well, clearly my life was a total time waster before knitting.

Your enlightened friend,
Alice

May 5

Dear Alice,

The sweater is fabulous, and I have to tell you
that it's been a pleasure watching you fall down
knitting's rabbit hole these past months, but I'm
correcting you on one thing: You already are a
Knitter with a capital K.

Being a Knitter versus being a knitter is not a
difference of competency and has nothing to do with
how good your sweaters look or how much yarn is in
the closet. It has to do with whether you know how
to knit and do it sometimes or whether knitting
has become a personality trait for you. I realized
that I was a Knitter many years ago, when I was
working on a sweater that had stopped being fun.
It was awful. I'd made a huge and obvious mistake
and I'd dropped down that section of stitches,
intending to fix the cable and knit it all back
up again, although things were going very wrong.
Somehow dropping the stitches back created extra
stitches and one of them wouldn't pick back up
again. That one stitch ran back to the cable before
that and I totally arsed up the whole thing and
I realized, as I was pulling back the whole damn
front of the sweater, that I wasn't having fun but
— significantly — that I wasn't stopping, either.
I had the option of taking that sweater out back
to the barbecue and straightening the whole thing
out with half a can of kerosene and a lighter, but
instead here I was, in a grudge match with some
knitting, determined to win.

I realized in that moment that I wasn't a knitter any longer. I wasn't someone who knit for fun and good times. I was suddenly a Knitter, and I was willing to do things that were hard and not fun and even truly difficult because knitting wasn't just a fun hobby for me anymore. It was an avocation, a calling, a personality trait. Knitting was feeding more than my need for a distraction; it was fulfilling some need to accomplish something myself with my own two hands.

I was so proud of that sweater. I was as proud of that sweater as you are of this one, and that makes both of us Knitters.

Fondly, as ever,

Marg

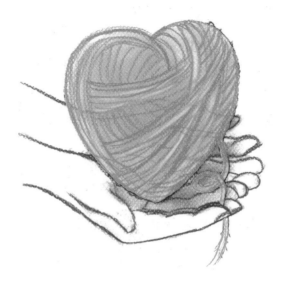

Things I Found in the Land of Knitting

- **Patience.** Knitting has taught me to sit nicely, listen well, and give things time. Knitting is slow, like love, baking bread, making good children, and other things that take a long time to pay off.
- **Hope.** Knitting can crash and burn and rise from the ashes, and in knitting there's always a way to work it out. You can make a sweater that fits no human, accept defeat, rip it back, and try the whole thing over again and get something that works. (This has been useful as I learn to be good at marriage, which is all about taking the same stuff and making it work a new way over and over again.)
- **Faith.** Twelve balls of yarn becomes a warm sweater. Three skeins of gossamer wool becomes a lace stole. One length of

wool darns my socks. My unruly girl children become adept young women. Knitting teaches a leap of faith. What you start with is not what you end with. Hang tough.

If you've done this trip right, you'll leave behind a great deal when you depart this earth. Every knitter leaves her legacy, a great swath of knitted stuff she churned out. And each knitter also leaves behind her stash — a pile of yarn, needles, and patterns that proves the knitter was here and speaks to the nature of her days while she knit, breathed, and loved on the earth. We know it looks like yarn, but it's not. We know it looks like an obsessive-compulsive disorder, but it's not. It's hope, it's good wishes, it's love and possibility and everything we ever thought we could make. It's how warm we wish we could have made you, it's how much time we wish we could have given you.

We know
it looks like yarn,
but it's love . . .
and for this
it's worth giving up all
your closet space.

ACKNOWLEDGMENTS

A THOUSAND THANKS to the Storey team, who always turn my words into such beautiful books: editor Deborah Balmuth, who earned extra points in this author's book for not losing her cool when I announced (a few months into the manuscript) that I was trashing the whole thing for a "travel book about knitting"; editor Elaine Cissi, who came to understand (over time) the true meaning and significance of the ellipses; Mary Velgos and Jamie Hogan for the incredible art direction and illustration that made this book everything I'd imagined and more; and special thanks to Pam Art for never calling me crazy, even when my ideas sound that way.

My agent, Linda Roghaar, deserves a gold star for her unfailing support and unsinkable good sense.

To my husband Joe and our daughters Amanda, Megan and Sam: my thanks for being there as well as for trying not to be there once the book got underway. (I know you tried to stay out of my office.) I love the bunch of you.

Gratitude to my brother Ian, who started this whole ball rolling when he loaned me his copy of *The Lonely Planet Guide to Costa Rica*.

Honorable mention, as always, to my mum, Bonnie; my sisters Erin and Ali; my nephew Hank; and my dear friends Lene and Ken, who keep me rooted to this spot as they inspire me to be more all the time. This is why I knit you guys socks.